Financial Accounting

Workbook

AAT Diploma Pathway Unit 5

D1422002

David Cox

osborne
BOOKS

Published by Osborne Books Limited
Unit 1B Everoak Estate
Bromyard Road
Worcester WR2 5HP
Tel 01905 748071
Email books@osbornebooks.co.uk
Website www.osbornebooks.co.uk

Design by Richard Holt
Cover image from Getty Images

Printed by the Bath Press, Bath

British Library Cataloguing in Publication Data
A catalogue record for this book is available from the British Library

ISBN 1 905777 07 8

Contents

Acknowledgements

The author wishes to thank the following for their help with the editing and production of the book: Jean Cox, Michael Fardon, Mike Gilbert, Rosemarie Griffiths, Claire McCarthy, and Jon Moore. Special thanks go to Roger Petheram, Series Editor, for reading, checking and advising on the development of the text. The publisher is indebted to the Association of Accounting Technicians for its generous help and advice to the author and editor during the preparation of this text, and for permission to reproduce sample assessment material.

Author

David Cox has more than twenty years' experience teaching accountancy students over a wide range of levels. Formerly with the Management and Professional Studies Department at Worcester College of Technology, he now lectures on a freelance basis and carries out educational consultancy work in accountancy studies. He is author and joint author of a number of textbooks in the areas of accounting, finance and banking.

Introduction

Financial Accounting Workbook is designed to be used alongside Osborne Books'
Financial Records and Accounts Tutorial and is ideal for student use in the classroom,
at home and on distance learning courses. Both the *Tutorial* and the *Workbook* are
designed for students preparing for assessment for Unit 5.

Financial Accounting Workbook is divided into two sections: Workbook Activities and
Practice Examinations.

Workbook Activities

Workbook activities are self-contained exercises which are designed to be used to
supplement the activities in the tutorial text. A number of them are more extended than
the exercises in the tutorial and provide useful practice for students preparing for the
Examination.

Practice Examinations

Osborne Books is grateful to the AAT for their kind permission for the reproduction
of the AAT Specimen Examination in this section and selected tasks from other
Examinations.

answers

The answers to the tasks and exams in the *Workbook* are available in a separate *Tutor
Pack*. Contact the Osborne Books Sales Office on 01905 748071 for further details.

www.osbornebooks.co.uk

Visit the Osborne Books website, which contains Resources sections for tutors and
students. These sections provide a wealth of free material, including downloadable
documents and layouts and assistance with other areas of study.

Workbook activities

This section contains activities which are suitable for use with the individual chapters of *Financial Records and Accounts Tutorial* from Osborne Books.

Photocopiable documents you will need, such as ledger accounts, extended trial balance, trial balance, trading and profit and loss account, balance sheet, journal pages and fixed asset registers, are to be found in the Appendix at the back of this Workbook.

1 THE ACCOUNTING SYSTEM

1.1 Write out and complete the following:

(a) The .... accountant is mainly concerned with external reporting.

(b) The sales day book is an example of a book of ....

(c) Sales ledger contains the personal accounts of ....

(d) Sales account is contained in the .... ledger.

(e) Income minus .... equals ....

(f) .... minus .... equals capital.

1.2 In an accounting system, which one of the following represents the most logical sequence?

(a) book of prime entry; prime document; double-entry book-keeping; trial balance; final accounts

(b) prime document; book of prime entry; double-entry book-keeping; trial balance; final accounts

(c) prime document; book of prime entry; double-entry book-keeping; final accounts; trial balance

(d) prime document; double-entry book-keeping, book of prime entry; trial balance; final accounts

Answer (a) or (b) or (c) or (d)

1.3   Write out the figures which make up the accounting equation (assets – liabilities = capital) after each of the following consecutive transactions (ignore VAT):

- owner starts in business with capital of £10,000 comprising £9,000 in the bank and £1,000 in cash

- buys office equipment for £2,500, paying by cheque

- obtains a loan of £2,000 by cheque from a friend

- buys factory machinery for £8,000, paying by cheque

- buys office equipment for £2,000 on credit from Wyvern Office Supplies

1.4   Fill in the missing figures:

	Assets £	Liabilities £	Capital £
(a)	10,000	0	....
(b)	20,000	7,500	....
(c)	16,750	....	10,500
(d)	....	4,350	12,680
(e)	17,290	....	11,865
(f)	....	6,709	17,294

1.5   The table below sets out account balances from the books of a business. The columns (a) to (f) show the account balances resulting from a series of transactions that have taken place over time. You are to compare each set of adjacent columns, ie (a) with (b) with (c), and so on, and state, with figures, what accounting transactions have taken place in each case. (Ignore VAT).

	(a)	(b)	(c)	(d)	(e)	(f)
	£	£	£	£	£	£
Assets						
Office equipment	–	5,000	5,000	5,500	5,500	5,500
Machinery	–	–	–	–	6,000	6,000
Bank	7,000	2,000	7,000	7,000	1,000	3,000
Cash	1,000	1,000	1,000	500	500	500
Liabilities						
Loan	–	–	5,000	5,000	5,000	5,000
Capital	8,000	8,000	8,000	8,000	8,000	10,000

2 DOUBLE-ENTRY BOOK-KEEPING

Note: a set of photocopiable blank ledger accounts is printed in the Appendix.

2.1 Fill in the missing words to the following sentences:

(a) A .... entry records an account which gains value, or records an asset, or an expense.

(b) In the books of a business, the .... side of bank account records money paid out.

(c) In capital account, the initial capital contributed by the owner of the business is recorded on the .... side.

(d) Office equipment is an example of a .... asset.

(e) The purchase of a photocopier for use in the office is classed as .... expenditure.

(f) Repairs to a photocopier are classed as .... expenditure.

2.2 The following are the business transactions of Andrew King (who is not registered for VAT) for the month of October 2004:

1 Oct	Started in business with capital of £7,500 in the bank
4 Oct	Bought a machine for £4,000, paying by cheque
6 Oct	Bought office equipment for £2,250, paying by cheque
11 Oct	Paid rent £400, by cheque
12 Oct	Obtained a loan of £1,500 from a friend, Tina Richards, and paid her cheque into the bank
15 Oct	Paid wages £500, by cheque
18 Oct	Commission received £200, by cheque
20 Oct	Drawings £250, by cheque
25 Oct	Paid wages £450, by cheque

You are to:

(a) write up Andrew King's bank account

(b) complete the double-entry book-keeping transactions

2.3 Write short notes, distinguishing between:

- (a) capital expenditure and revenue expenditure
- (b) debit balance and credit balance
- (c) bank account and cash account
- (d) capital account and drawings account

2.4 The purchase of goods for resale on credit is recorded in the accounts as:

	Debit	Credit
(a)	creditor's account	purchases account
(b)	purchases account	cash account
(c)	purchases account	creditor's account
(d)	creditor's account	sales account

Answer (a) or (b) or (c) or (d)

2.5 Unsatisfactory goods, which were purchased on credit, are returned to the supplier. This is recorded in the accounts as:

	Debit	Credit
(a)	sales returns account	creditor's account
(b)	purchases returns account	creditor's account
(c)	creditor's account	purchases returns account
(d)	creditor's account	purchases account

Answer (a) or (b) or (c) or (d)

2.6 Write short notes, distinguishing between:

- (a) cash purchases and credit purchases
- (b) sales and sales returns
- (c) carriage inwards and carriage outwards
- (d) discount allowed and discount received

2.7 For each transaction below, complete the table to show the accounts which will be debited and credited:

(a) Bought goods, paying by cheque

(b) Cheque received for cash sales

(c) Bought goods on credit from Teme Traders

(d) Sold goods on credit to L Harris

(e) Returned unsatisfactory goods to Teme Traders

(f) L Harris returns unsatisfactory goods

(g) Received a loan from D Perkins, by cheque

(h) Withdrew cash from the bank for use in the business

Transaction	Account debited	Account credited
(a)		
(b)		
(c)		
(d)		
(e)		
(f)		
(g)		
(h)		

Note: ignore Value Added Tax

2.8   The following are the business transactions of Pershore Packaging for the month of January 2004:

4 Jan   Bought goods, £250, on credit from AB Supplies Limited

5 Jan   Sold goods, £195, a cheque being received

7 Jan   Sold goods, £150, cash being received

11 Jan   Received a loan of £1,000 from J Johnson by cheque

15 Jan   Paid £250 to AB Supplies Limited by cheque

18 Jan   Sold goods, £145, on credit to L Lewis

20 Jan   Bought goods, £225, paying by cheque

22 Jan   Paid wages, £125, in cash

26 Jan   Bought office equipment, £160, on credit from Mercia Office Supplies Limited

28 Jan   Received a cheque for £145 from L Lewis

29 Jan   Paid the amount owing to Mercia Office Supplies Limited by cheque

You are to record the transactions in the books of account.

Notes:

• *Pershore Packaging is not registered for Value Added Tax*

• *day books are not required*

2.9   Enter the following transactions into the double-entry accounts of Sonya Smith:

2004

2 Feb   Bought goods £200, on credit from G Lewis

4 Feb   Sold goods £150, on credit to L Jarvis

8 Feb   Sold goods £240, on credit to G Patel

10 Feb   Paid G Lewis the amount owing by cheque after deducting a settlement discount of 5%

12 Feb   L Jarvis pays the amount owing by cheque after deducting a settlement discount of 2%

17 Feb   Bought goods £160, on credit from G Lewis

19 Feb   G Patel pays the amount owing by cheque after deducting a settlement discount of 2.5%

24 Feb   Paid G Lewis the amount owing by cheque after deducting a settlement discount of 5%

Notes:

• *Sonya Smith is not registered for Value Added Tax*

• *day books are not required*

3 BALANCING ACCOUNTS AND THE TRIAL BALANCE

Note: a set of photocopiable blank ledger accounts is printed in the Appendix.

3.1   Which one of the following accounts normally has a debit balance?

    (a)   loan

    (b)   bank overdraft

    (c)   sales

    (d)   purchases

    Answer (a) or (b) or (c) or (d)

3.2   Which one of the following accounts normally has a credit balance?

    (a)   drawings

    (b)   capital

    (c)   cash

    (d)   premises

    Answer (a) or (b) or (c) or (d)

3.3   Produce the trial balance of Tina Wong as at 30 November 2004. She has omitted to open a capital account.

	£
Bank overdraft	1,855
Capital	?
Cash	85
Creditors	1,082
Debtors	2,115
Equipment	2,500
Purchases	2,419
Purchases returns	102
Sales	4,164
Sales returns	354
Van	7,500
Wages	1,230

3.4 The book-keeper of Lorna Fox has extracted the following list of balances as at 31 March 2004:

	£
Administration expenses	10,240
Bank overdraft	1,050
Capital	155,440
Cash	150
Creditors	10,545
Debtors	10,390
Drawings	9,450
Interest paid	2,350
Loan from bank	20,000
Machinery	40,000
Premises	125,000
Purchases	96,250
Sales	146,390
Sales returns	8,500
Telephone	3,020
Travel expenses	1,045
Value Added Tax (amount due)	1,950
Wages	28,980

You are to:

(a) Produce the trial balance at 31 March 2004.

(b) Take any three debit balances and any three credit balances and explain to someone who does not understand accounting why they are listed as such, and what this means to the business.

3.5   Fill in the missing words from the following sentences:

(a)   "You made an error of .... when you debited the cost of diesel

fuel for the van to vans account."

(b)   "I've had the book-keeper from D Jones Limited on the 'phone concerning the statements of

account that we sent out the other day. She says that there is a sales invoice charged that

she knows nothing about. I wonder if we have done a .... and it should

be for T Jones' account?"

(c)   "There is a 'bad figure' on a purchases invoice – we have read it as £35 when it should be

£55. It has gone through our accounts wrongly so we have an error of ....

.... to put right."

(d)   "Although the trial balance balanced last week, I've since found an error of £100 in the

calculation of the balance of sales account. We will need to check the other balances as I

think we may have a .... error."

(e)   "Who was in charge of that trainee last week? He has entered the payment for the electricity

bill on the debit side of the bank and on the credit side of electricity – a ....

of ...."

(f)   "I found this purchase invoice from last week in amongst the copy letters. As we haven't put

it through the accounts we have an error of ...."

3.6 The following are the business transactions of Mark Tansall, a retailer of computer software, for the months of January and February 2004:

Transactions for January

2004

1 Jan	Started in business with capital of £10,000 in the bank
4 Jan	Paid rent on premises £500, by cheque
5 Jan	Bought shop fittings £5,000, by cheque
7 Jan	Bought stock of software, £7,500, on credit from Tech Software
11 Jan	Software sales £2,400, paid into bank
12 Jan	Software sales £2,000, paid into bank
16 Jan	Bought software £5,000, on credit from Datasoft Limited
20 Jan	Software sales £1,500 to Wyvern School, a cheque being received
22 Jan	Software sales £2,250, paid into bank
25 Jan	Bought software from A & A Supplies £3,000, by cheque
27 Jan	Wyvern School returned software £280, cheque refund sent
29 Jan	Sold software on credit to Teme College, £2,495

Transactions for February

2004

2 Feb	Software sales £2,720, paid into bank
4 Feb	Paid rent on premises £500, by cheque
5 Feb	Bought shop fittings £1,550, by cheque
10 Feb	Software sales £3,995, paid into bank
12 Feb	Sent cheque, £7,500, to Tech Software

15 Feb   Bought software £4,510, on credit from Tech Software

19 Feb   Sent cheque, £5,000, to Datasoft Limited

22 Feb   Software sales £1,930, paid into bank

23 Feb   Teme College returned software, £145

24 Feb   Software sales £2,145, paid into bank

25 Feb   Bought software £2,120, on credit from Associated Software

26 Feb   Software sales £4,150, paid into bank

You are to:

(a)   Record the January transactions in the books of account, and balance each account at 31 January 2004.

(b)   Draw up a trial balance at 31 January 2004.

(c)   Record the February transactions in the books of account, and balance each account at 29 February 2004.

(d)   Draw up a trial balance at 29 February 2004.

Notes:

*   *Mark Tansall is not registered for Value Added Tax*
*   *day books are not required*
*   *Mark Tansall's accounting system does not use control accounts*
*   *make sure that you leave plenty of space for each account – particularly sales, purchases and bank*

4 FINAL ACCOUNTS – THE EXTENDED TRIAL BALANCE

Extended trial balance format

A blank photocopiable extended trial balance is included in the Appendix – it is advisable to enlarge it up to full A4 size. Alternatively you can set up a computer spreadsheet – but remember to allow for all the rows shown on the pro-forma – they will be needed in later Workbook Activities.

4.1 Which one of the following does not appear in the profit and loss account?

(a) closing stock

(b) purchases

(c) interest paid

(d) cash

Answer (a) or (b) or (c) or (d)

4.2 Which one of the following does not appear in the balance sheet?

(a) closing stock

(b) sales

(c) debtors

(d) bank

Answer (a) or (b) or (c) or (d)

4.3   The following trial balance has been extracted by the book-keeper of Matt Smith at 31 December 2004:

	Dr £	Cr £
Opening stock	14,350	
Purchases	114,472	
Sales		259,688
Rates	13,718	
Heating and lighting	12,540	
Wages and salaries	42,614	
Motor vehicle expenses	5,817	
Advertising	6,341	
Premises	75,000	
Office equipment	33,000	
Motor vehicles	21,500	
Debtors	23,854	
Bank	1,235	
Cash	125	
Capital		62,500
Drawings	12,358	
Loan from bank		35,000
Creditors		14,258
Value Added Tax		5,478
	376,924	376,924

Note: closing stock was valued at £16,280

You are to prepare the final accounts of Matt Smith for the year ended 31 December 2004, using the extended trial balance method.

Note: please retain the extended trial balance as it will be used on page 25 as the starting point for a further Workbook Activity.

4.4   The following trial balance has been extracted by the book-keeper of Clare Lewis at 31 December 2004:

	Dr	Cr
	£	£
Debtors	18,600	
Creditors		11,480
Value Added Tax		1,870
Bank overdraft		4,610
Capital		25,250
Sales		144,810
Purchases	96,318	
Opening stock	16,010	
Salaries	18,465	
Heating and lighting	1,820	
Rent and rates	5,647	
Motor vehicles	9,820	
Office equipment	5,500	
Sundry expenses	845	
Motor vehicle expenses	1,684	
Drawings	13,311	
Closing stock – trading and profit & loss account		13,735
Closing stock – balance sheet	13,735	
	201,755	201,755

Tutorial note: this trial balance already incorporates the closing stock adjustments.

You are to prepare the final accounts of Clare Lewis for the year ended 31 December 2004, using the extended trial balance method.

Note: please retain the extended trial balance as it will be used on page 25 as the starting point for a further Workbook Activity.

4.5 The trial balance of Jane Richardson, who runs a secretarial agency, has been prepared at 31 December 2004 as follows:

	Dr	Cr
	£	£
Capital		25,000
Office equipment	30,000	
Income from clients		75,450
Administration expenses	3,280	
Wages	37,145	
Rent paid	8,052	
Telephone	1,287	
Travel expenses	926	
Rates	2,355	
Debtors	3,698	
Creditors		1,074
Value Added Tax		2,021
Bank	3,971	
Cash	241	
Drawings	12,590	
	103,545	103,545

You are to prepare the final accounts of Jane Richardson for the year ended 31 December 2004, using the extended trial balance method.

Note: please retain the extended trial balance as it will be used on page 25 as the starting point for a further Workbook Activity.

5 SOLE TRADER FINAL ACCOUNTS

Conventional format

Example layouts of the trading and profit and loss account and balance sheet in conventional format – or proper form – are included in the Appendix. They may be photocopied for guidance with Workbook Activities; alternatively, a computer spreadsheet layout can be set up.

5.1   Cost of sales is calculated as:

    (a)   opening stock + purchases – closing stock

    (b)   purchases – opening stock + closing stock

    (c)   opening stock + purchases + closing stock

    (d)   purchases – opening stock – closing stock

    Answer (a) or (b) or (c) or (d)

5.2   Which one of the following is used to calculate net profit?

    (a)   trial balance

    (b)   trading account

    (c)   balance sheet

    (d)   profit and loss account

    Answer (a) or (b) or (c) or (d)

5.3   Which one of the following describes working capital?

    (a)   the excess of fixed assets over long-term liabilities

    (b)   the excess of current assets over long-term liabilities

    (c)   the excess of current assets over current liabilities

    (d)   the excess of fixed assets over current liabilities

    Answer (a) or (b) or (c) or (d)

5.4 You are to fill in the missing figures for the following sole trader businesses:

	Sales	Opening stock	Purchases	Closing stock	Gross profit	Overheads	Net profit or loss*
	£	£	£	£	£	£	£
Business A	20,000	5,000	10,000	3,000	....	4,000	....
Business B	35,000	8,000	15,000	5,000	....	....	10,000
Business C	....	6,500	18,750	7,250	18,500	11,750	....
Business D	45,250	9,500	....	10,500	20,750	....	10,950
Business E	71,250	....	49,250	9,100	22,750	24,450	....
Business F	25,650	4,950	13,750	....	11,550	....	(3,450)

* Note: net loss is indicated by brackets

5.5 *Please refer back to the extended trial balance of Matt Smith prepared in Workbook Activity 4.3.*

You are to prepare the final accounts of Matt Smith for the year ended 31 December 2004 in proper form, using the conventional format.

5.6 *Please refer back to the extended trial balance of Clare Lewis prepared in Workbook Activity 4.4.*

You are to prepare the final accounts of Clare Lewis for the year ended 31 December 2004 in proper form, using the conventional format.

5.7 *Please refer back to the extended trial balance of Jane Richardson prepared in Workbook Activity 4.5.*

You are to prepare the final accounts of Jane Richardson for the year ended 31 December 2004 in proper form, using the conventional format.

6 ACCRUALS AND PREPAYMENTS

Extended trial balance format

A blank photocopiable pro-forma of the extended trial balance is included in the Appendix – it is advisable to enlarge it up to full A4 size.

Conventional format

Blank photocopiable pro-formas of the trading and profit and loss account and balance sheet are included in the Appendix – it is advisable to enlarge them up to full A4 size.

6.1 Show how the following will be recorded in the accounts of a business with a financial year end of 31 December 2004.

(a) Rent paid for the business premises is £500 per month. The rental for January 2005 was paid in December 2004 and is included in the total payments during 2004 which amounted to £6,500.

(b) Motor vehicle expenses paid to 31 December 2004 amount to £8,455. On 4 January 2005 a fuel bill of £610 is received which relates to December. The bill is paid by cheque on 18 January 2005.

(c) A claim has been made on the company's insurance policy for stock damaged in a small fire. On 16 December 2004, the amount of the claim has been agreed at £180. The amount is paid by the insurance company on 26 January 2005.

(d) At 31 December 2004, the balance of telephone account is £500. Of this, £100 is the amount of personal calls made by the owner of the business.

6.2 Write short notes distinguishing between *income and expenditure accounting* and *receipts and payments accounting*.

6.3 A credit balance on accruals account indicates:

(a)   a liability and an expense owing

(b)   an asset and a prepayment of income

(c)   an asset and an accrual of income

(d)   a liability and an expense prepaid

Answer (a) or (b) or (c) or (d)

6.4 Which one of the following is a current asset?

(a)   creditors

(b)   accruals

(c)   machinery

(d)   prepayments

Answer (a) or (b) or (c) or (d)

6.5   The following trial balance has been extracted by the book-keeper of Cindy Hayward, who runs a delicatessen shop, at 30 June 2004:

	Dr	Cr
	£	£
Capital		20,932
Drawings	10,000	
Purchases	148,500	
Sales		210,900
Repairs to buildings	848	
Delivery van	5,000	
Van expenses	1,540	
Land and buildings	85,000	
Loan from bank		60,000
Bank	540	
Shop fittings	2,560	
Wages and salaries	30,280	
Discount allowed	135	
Discount received		1,319
Rates and insurance	2,690	
Debtors	3,175	
Creditors		8,295
Heating and lighting	3,164	
General expenses	4,680	
Sales returns	855	
Purchases returns		1,221
Opening stock	6,210	
Value Added Tax		2,510
Closing stock – trading and profit & loss account		7,515
Closing stock – balance sheet	7,515	
	312,692	312,692

Notes at 30 June 2004:
- rates prepaid £255
- wages owing £560
- van expenses owing £85
- goods costing £200 were taken by Cindy Hayward for her own use

You are to prepare the final accounts of Cindy Hayward for the year ended 30 June 2004:
- using the extended trial balance method
- in proper form, using the conventional format

6.6 The following list of balances has been extracted by the book-keeper of Southtown Supplies, a wholesaling business, at 31 December 2004:

	£
Opening stock	70,000
Purchases	280,000
Sales	420,000
Sales returns	6,000
Purchases returns	4,500
Discount received	750
Discount allowed	500
Electricity	13,750
Salaries	35,600
Post and packing	1,400
Premises	120,000
Fixtures and fittings	45,000
Debtors	55,000
Creditors	47,000
Bank balance	5,000
Capital	195,000
Drawings	41,000
Value Added Tax (amount due)	6,000

Notes at 31 December 2004:

- stock was valued at £60,000; this figure excludes goods which were damaged by a burst water pipe and have been scrapped (no sale proceeds); Wyvern Insurance has agreed to cover the loss of £500 incurred in writing off the goods

- electricity owing £350

- salaries prepaid £400

You are to prepare the final accounts of Southtown Supplies for the year ended 31 December 2004:

- using the extended trial balance method

- in proper form, using the conventional format

7 DEPRECIATION OF FIXED ASSETS

Extended trial balance format

A blank photocopiable pro-forma of the extended trial balance is included in the Appendix – it is advisable to enlarge it up to full A4 size.

Conventional format

Blank photocopiable pro-formas of the trading and profit and loss account and balance sheet are included in the Appendix – it is advisable to enlarge them up to full A4 size.

7.1 A car which cost £20,000 is being depreciated at 30 per cent per year using the reducing balance method. At the end of three years it will have a net book value of:

(a) £2,000

(b) £6,860

(c) £13,140

(d) £18,000

Answer (a) or (b) or (c) or (d)

7.2 A car is being depreciated using the reducing balance method. The original cost of the car was £15,000. At the end of year three it has a net book value of £5,145. What percentage of reducing balance is being used?

(a) 20%

(b) 25%

(c) 30%

(d) 35%

Answer (a) or (b) or (c) or (d)

7.3 A machine which originally cost £1,000 is sold for £350 (both amounts net of VAT). The provision for depreciation account for this machine shows a balance of £620. This means (for a VAT-registered business) that there is a:

(a) loss on sale of £380

(b) profit on sale of £350

(c) loss on sale of £30

(d) profit on sale of £30

Answer (a) or (b) or (c) or (d)

7.4 The book-keeping entries to record a profit on sale of fixed assets are:

	Debit	Credit
(a)	fixed asset account	profit and loss account
(b)	disposals account	profit and loss account
(c)	profit and loss account	disposals account
(d)	bank account	profit and loss account

Answer (a) or (b) or (c) or (d)

7.5 Martin Hough, sole owner of Juicyburger, a fast food shop, operating from leased premises in the town, is suspicious of his accountant, Mr S Harris, whom he claims doesn't really understand the food business. On the telephone he asks Mr Harris why depreciation is charged on a rigid formula, as surely no-one really knows how much his equipment is worth, and in fact he might not get anything for it. Draft a reply to Mr Hough from Mr Harris explaining the importance of depreciation and its application to final accounts.

7.6 Rachael Hall's financial year runs to 31 December. On 1 January 2004, her accounts show that she owns a car with an original cost of £12,000 and depreciation to date of £7,200.

On 1 October 2004, Rachael bought a new car at a cost of £15,000. She traded in the old car at a part-exchange value of £5,500 and paid the balance by cheque.

Rachael depreciates vehicles at 20 per cent per year using the straight-line method. Her accounting policy is to charge a full year's depreciation in the year of purchase, but none in the year of sale.

You are to show:

(a) vehicles account for 2004

(b) depreciation account for 2004

(c) provision for depreciation account for 2004

(d) asset disposal account for 2004

(e) balance sheet extract at 31 December 2004

7.7 The following trial balance has been extracted by the book-keeper of Wintergreen Supplies at 31 December 2004:

	Dr	Cr
	£	£
Premises at cost	120,000	
Provision for depreciation (premises)		7,200
Long-term loan		52,800
Capital		70,000
Debtors	1,900	
Creditors		1,500
Drawings	6,750	
Cash	150	
Opening stock	4,200	
Fixtures and fittings at cost	5,000	
Provision for depreciation (fixtures and fittings)		1,000
Vehicles at cost	10,000	
Provision for depreciation (vehicles)		2,000
Bank		750
Sales		195,000
Purchases	154,000	
Wages	20,500	
Sundry expenses	9,500	
Value Added Tax		1,750
Closing stock – trading and profit & loss account		5,200
Closing stock – balance sheet	5,200	
	337,200	337,200

Notes at 31 December 2004:

- premises are to be depreciated at 2 per cent (straight-line)

- vehicles and fixtures and fittings are to be depreciated at 20 per cent (straight-line)

- wages prepaid are £560, and sundry expenses accrued are £500

You are to prepare the final accounts of Wintergreen Supplies for the year ended 31 December 2004:

- using the extended trial balance method

- in proper form, using the conventional format

7.8 Cindy Smith owns an engineering supplies business, and the following trial balance has been extracted by her book-keeper at 30 June 2004:

	Dr	Cr
	£	£
Capital		38,825
Opening stock	18,050	
Purchases	74,280	
Sales		149,410
Discounts	3,210	1,140
Rent and rates	7,280	
Returns	1,645	875
Cash	820	
Bank		13,300
Debtors and creditors	14,375	8,065
Wages and salaries	43,895	
General expenses	2,515	
Motor vehicles at cost	30,000	
Provision for depreciation on motor vehicles		7,500
Fixtures and fittings at cost	10,000	
Provision for depreciation on fixtures and fittings		3,000
Motor vehicle expenses	6,725	
Drawings	12,500	
Value Added Tax		3,180
	225,295	225,295

Notes at 30 June 2004:

- stock was valued at £20,145
- general expenses owing £175
- rates prepaid £95
- depreciate motor vehicles at 25 per cent per annum, using the reducing balance method
- depreciate fixtures and fittings at 10 per cent per annum, using the straight-line method

You are to prepare the final accounts of Cindy Smith for the year ended 30 June 2004:

- using the extended trial balance method
- in proper form, using the conventional format

8 BAD DEBTS AND PROVISION FOR DOUBTFUL DEBTS

Extended trial balance format

A blank photocopiable pro-forma of the extended trial balance is included in the Appendix – it is advisable to enlarge it up to full A4 size.

Conventional format

Blank photocopiable pro-formas of the trading and profit and loss account and balance sheet are included in the Appendix – it is advisable to enlarge them up to full A4 size.

8.1 The accounts supervisor at the firm where you work has instructed you to write off a debtor's account as bad. Which one of the following double-entry book-keeping entries will you make?

	Debit	*Credit*
(a)	debtor's account	bad debts written off account
(b)	bank account	debtor's account
(c)	bad debts written off account	debtor's account
(d)	debtor's account	provision for doubtful debts account

Answer (a) or (b) or (c) or (d)

Ignore VAT relief on bad debt write-off.

8.2 An increase in provision for doubtful debts will:

(a) decrease net profit for the year

(b) be recorded in the debtors' accounts

(c) decrease the cash/bank balance

(d) increase net profit for the year

Answer (a) or (b) or (c) or (d)

8.3 The profit and loss account of a business has been prepared showing a net loss of £2,350. A reduction of £150 in the provision for doubtful debts should have been made, and bad debts of £70 should have been written off. Net loss will now be:

(a) £2,130

(b) £2,270

(c) £2,430

(d) £2,570

Answer (a) or (b) or (c) or (d)

Ignore VAT relief on bad debt write-off.

8.4 You are the book-keeper at Enterprise Trading Company. The following information is available for the financial years ending 31 December 2005, 2006, 2007:

	£
• Debtor balances at 31 December 2005, before writing off bad debts	105,200
• Bad debts written off on 31 December 2005	1,800
• 2.5% provision for doubtful debts created at 31 December 2005	
• Debtor balances at 31 December 2006, before writing off bad debts	115,600
• Bad debts written off on 31 December 2006	2,400
• 2.5% provision for doubtful debts adjusted in line with the change in the level of debtors at 31 December 2006	
• Debtor balances at 31 December 2007, before writing off bad debts	110,200
• Bad debts written off on 31 December 2007	1,400
• 2.5% provision for doubtful debts adjusted in line with the change in the level of debtors at 31 December 2007	

Note: ignore VAT relief on bad debt write-off

You are to:

(a) write up the following accounts for 2005, 2006 and 2007 (see pages 36 and 37):

– bad debts written off

– provision for doubtful debts: adjustment

– provision for doubtful debts

(b) show the effect of these transactions in the following table:

YEAR	PROFIT AND LOSS ACCOUNT				BALANCE SHEET		
	Expense		Income				
	Bad debts	Prov for doubtful debts	Bad debts	Prov for doubtful debts	Debtors	Less prov for doubtful debts	Net debtors
	£	£	£	£	£	£	£
2005							
2006							
2007							

Dr   **Bad Debts Written Off Account**   Cr

Date	Details	Amount	Date	Details	Amount
		£			£

Dr   **Provision for Doubtful Debts: Adjustment Account**   Cr

Date	Details	Amount	Date	Details	Amount
		£			£

Dr   **Provision for Doubtful Debts Account**   Cr

Date	Details	Amount	Date	Details	Amount
		£			£

8.5 The following trial balance has been extracted by the book-keeper of Jane Jones, who sells carpets, as at 31 December 2005:

	Dr	Cr
	£	£
Debtors	37,200	
Creditors		30,640
Value Added Tax		4,280
Bank	14,640	
Capital		50,500
Sales		289,620
Purchases	182,636	
Opening stock	32,020	
Wages and salaries	36,930	
Heat and light	3,640	
Rent and rates	11,294	
Vehicles	20,000	
Provision for depreciation on vehicles		4,000
Equipment	10,000	
Provision for depreciation on equipment		1,000
Sundry expenses	1,690	
Motor expenses	3,368	
Drawings	26,622	
	380,040	380,040

Notes at 31 December 2005:

- stock was valued at £34,000
- bad debts of £2,200 are to be written off and a provision for doubtful debts of 5% is to be created
- vehicles are to be depreciated at 20% per annum and equipment at 10% per annum (both using the reducing balance method)
- there are sundry expenses accruals of £270, and rates prepayments of £2,190

You are to prepare the final accounts of Jane Jones for the year ended 31 December 2005:

- using the extended trial balance method
- in proper form, using the conventional format

8.6 The following trial balance has been extracted by the book-keeper of Andrew Brown, a fashion designer, as at 31 December 2005:

	Dr	Cr
	£	£
Purchases	31,480	
Sales		95,660
Opening stock	7,580	
Returns	240	620
Discounts	380	1,080
Drawings	34,720	
Premises at cost	100,000	
Provision for depreciation on premises		10,000
Fixtures and fittings	24,000	
Provision for depreciation on fixtures and fittings		3,000
Wages and salaries	18,620	
Advertising	2,260	
Rates	8,240	
Sundry expenses	7,390	
Bank	4,020	
Cash	120	
Debtors	5,000	
Bad debts written off	100	
Provision for doubtful debts		520
Creditors		3,740
Value Added Tax		3,240
Capital		81,290
Bank loan		45,000
	244,150	244,150

Notes at 31 December 2005:
- stock was valued at £6,060
- depreciate premises at 2 per cent using the straight-line method
- depreciate fixtures and fittings at 12.5 per cent per annum using the straight-line method
- provision for doubtful debts is to be 5% of debtors
- wages accrued are £500, and advertising prepaid is £350

You are to prepare the final accounts of Andrew Brown for the year ended 31 December 2005:
- using the extended trial balance method
- in proper form, using the conventional format

9 THE REGULATORY FRAMEWORK OF ACCOUNTING

9.1 (a) Explain the accounting concept of materiality.

(b) Describe three types of situation to which the concept of materiality is applicable.

(c) Suggest two problems which may occur when applying the concept of materiality.

9.2 Eveshore Electronics Limited imports electronic goods from the Far East and sells to retailers in the UK. The company has always valued its stock on the FIFO (first in, first out) basis. One of the directors comments that, because of the recent strength of the pound sterling against Far Eastern currencies, the price of imported electronic goods has been falling throughout the year. She suggests that the closing stock should be recalculated on the LIFO (last in, first out) basis.

(a) Assuming that the prices of electronic goods have been falling throughout the year, would the change suggested increase profit for the year, decrease profit, or would profit remain the same?

(b) Which accounting concept states that a business should not normally change its basis for valuing stock unless it has good reasons for so doing?

9.3 A business buys twenty units of a product in January at a cost of £3.00 each; it buys ten more in February at £3.50 each, and ten in April at £4.00 each. Eight units are sold in March, and sixteen are sold in May.

You are to calculate the value of closing stock at the end of May using:

(a) FIFO (first in, first out)

(b) LIFO (last in, first out)

(c) AVCO (average cost)

Note: where appropriate, work to the nearest penny.

9.4   Wyvern Office Supplies sells a range of pens, paper, computer supplies and other office sundries. One of its lines is photocopying paper for which the stock movements in January 2004 were:

1 January	Stock of 800 reams (a ream is 500 sheets) of photocopying paper brought forward at a cost of £2.00 per ream
5 January	Sold 700 reams
11 January	Bought 1,200 reams at £2.20 per ream
15 January	Sold 600 reams
19 January	Bought 1,000 reams at £2.10 per ream
21 January	Sold 400 reams
26 January	Bought 700 reams at £2.25 per ream

The selling price of each ream is £3.25.

You are to calculate the value of:

(a)   sales for January

(b)   the closing stock at 31 January and cost of sales for January, assuming that stock is valued on the FIFO (first in, first out) basis

(c)   the closing stock at 31 January and cost of sales for January, assuming that stock is valued on the LIFO (last in, first out) basis

9.5 YZ Limited is formed on 1 January 2004 and trades in two products, Y and Z. At the end of its first half-year the stock movements of the two products are as follows:

	PRODUCT Y		PRODUCT Z	
2004	Bought (units)	Sold (units)	Bought (units)	Sold (units)
January	100 at £4.00		200 at £10.00	
February		80 at £10.00	100 at £9.50	
March	140 at £4.20			240 at £16.00
April	100 at £3.80		100 at £10.50	
May		140 at £10.00	140 at £10.00	
June	80 at £4.50			100 at £16.00

The company values stock on the FIFO (first in, first out) basis.

At 30 June 2004, the net realisable value of each type of stock is:

product Y	£1,750.00
product Z	£1,950.00
	£3,700.00

You are to calculate the value of:

(a)   total sales for the half-year

(b)   the closing stock at 30 June 2004 for each product using the FIFO basis

(c)   the total at which the company's stocks should be valued on 30 June 2004 in order to comply with standard accounting practice

(d)   cost of sales for the half-year in order to comply with standard accounting practice

9.6 Which one of the following is revenue expenditure?

(a)   purchase of a computer for the office

(b)   legal costs for the purchase of property

(c)   cost of extension to property

(d)   quarterly electricity bill

Answer (a) or (b) or (c) or (d)

9.7 Which one of the following is capital expenditure?

(a) repairs to motor vehicles

(b) goods taken by owner for own use

(c) cost of raw materials used in extending the premises

(d) renewing the electrical wiring in the office

Answer (a) or (b) or (c) or (d)

9.8 Wages paid to own employees who have redecorated the office are:

(a) capital expenditure

(b) debited to profit and loss account

(d) debited to premises account

(d) credited to profit and loss account

Answer (a) or (b) or (c) or (d)

9.9 Classify the following costs (tick the appropriate column):

	capital expenditure	revenue expenditure
(a) purchase of motor vehicles		
(b) depreciation of motor vehicles		
(c) rent paid on premises		
(d) wages and salaries		
(e) legal fees relating to the purchase of property		
(f) re-decoration of office		
(g) installation of air-conditioning in office		
(h) wages of own employees used to build extension to the stockroom		
(i) installation and setting up of a new machine		

10 ACCOUNTING FOR CAPITAL TRANSACTIONS

10.1   Which one of the following is an intangible fixed asset?

(a)   vehicles

(b)   goodwill

(c)   hire purchase

(d)   premises

Answer (a) or (b) or (c) or (d)

10.2   Eveshore Enterprises is considering the use of hire purchase as a means of financing a new computer. Which of the following statements is correct?

(a)   at the end of the hire purchase contract, ownership of the computer will pass from the finance company to Eveshore Enterprises

(b)   a hire purchase contract is the same as an operating lease

(c)   at the end of the hire purchase contract, the finance company will collect the computer from Eveshore Enterprises

(d)   as the computer is being financed through hire purchase, it is not recorded on the balance sheet of Eveshore Enterprises

Answer (a) or (b) or (c) or (d)

10.3   (a)   An extract from the fixed asset register of Mereford Manufacturing is shown on the next page. You are to update the register with depreciation on the fixed asset for the years ended 31 December 2002 and 2003.

(b)   The fixed asset is sold on 20 April 2004 for £600 (net of VAT). The company does not charge depreciation in the year of sale. You are to complete the fixed asset register showing the machine's disposal.

EXTRACT FROM FIXED ASSET REGISTER

Description/serial no	Date acquired	Original cost £	Depreciation £	NBV £	Funding method	Disposal proceeds £	Disposal date
Machinery							
Moulding machine	7/2/00	10,000.00			Cash		
Year ended 31/12/00			2,000.00	8,000.00			
Year ended 31/12/01			2,000.00	6,000.00			

10.4   Perham Publishing, which has a financial year end of 31 December, bought a colour laser printer on 11 February 2002 at a cost of £2,000 (paid by cheque). The printer is expected to last for four years, after which its estimated value will be £260. Depreciation is charged at 40 per cent each year using the reducing balance method; it is charged in full in the year of purchase, but not in the year of sale.

The printer is part-exchanged for a more up-to-date model on 19 October 2004. The part-exchange allowance is £400.

You are to

(a)   show the accounting entries (journal and cash book not required) to record the acquisition, depreciation and disposal of the printer for the years 2002, 2003, 2004.

   Note: VAT is to be ignored

(b)   draw up a page from the fixed asset register to show the printer's acquisition, depreciation and disposal. (A photocopiable page from the fixed asset register is provided in the Appendix).

10.5   John and Sara Smith run a delivery company called 'J & S Transport'. They started in business on 1 January 2002 with two vans which cost £16,000 each (paid by cheque). On 1 January 2004, a further two vans were bought at a cost of £18,000 each (paid by cheque) and, on 20 March 2004, one of the original vans was sold for £8,000 (cheque received).

Depreciation is charged at 25 per cent each year using the reducing balance method; depreciation is charged in the year of purchase, but none in the year of sale.

The Smith's financial year end is 31 December.

You are to show the accounting entries (journal and cash book not required) to record the acquisition, depreciation and disposal of vans for the years 2002, 2003 and 2004.

Notes:

•   VAT is to be ignored

•   use one fixed asset account for all vans, one depreciation account and one provision for depreciation account

10.6   (a)   Write short notes, distinguishing between:

   •   an operating lease

   •   a finance lease

(b)   Explain the accounting treatment of each of these types of lease in the accounts of the lessee (the person to whom the asset is leased).

11 CONTROL ACCOUNTS

11.1 Would the following errors cause a difference between the balance of the sales ledger control account and the total of the balances in the sales ledger?

(a)   The sales returns day book was undercast by £100.

(b)   The amount of a credit note issued was credited to the account of Martley Traders instead of Martley Manufacturing.

11.2 On 31 December 2004 the balances of the creditor accounts in the subsidiary (purchases) ledger of Thomas Limited were listed, totalled, and compared with the balance of the purchases ledger control account. The total of the list of creditor balances amounted to £55,946. Investigations were carried out and the following errors were discovered:

(a)   a creditor balance of £553 had been listed as £535

(b)   settlement discount received of £100 had been credited to the creditor's account

(c)   a credit note received for £141 (including VAT) had not been recorded in the creditor's account

(d)   a creditor balance of £225 had been listed twice

You are to record the appropriate adjustments in the table below; show clearly the amount involved and whether it is to be added or subtracted.

		£
Total of list of creditor balances		55,946
Adjustment for (a)	add/subtract	....
Adjustment for (b)	add/subtract	....
Adjustment for (c)	add/subtract	....
Adjustment for (d)	add/subtract	....
Revised total to agree with purchases ledger control account		....

11.3   The following accounts, together with their balances at 1 January 2004, form the subsidiary (purchases) ledger of A Austin:

B Bedford   £596.41

C Chrysler   £602.03

D De Lorean   £228.14

F Ford   £487.29

During January the following transactions took place:

  5 Jan   Bought goods on credit from C Chrysler £127.55 and from F Ford £298.31

  7 Jan   Bought goods on credit from B Bedford £348.19 and from D De Lorean £422.19

  11 Jan   Returned goods to C Chrysler £12.34 and to B Bedford £59.68

  15 Jan   Paid D De Lorean £250.00 on account, by cheque

  21 Jan   Paid F Ford by cheque the balance owing on the account after deducting a 5% cash discount

You are to:

(a)   write up the accounts in the subsidiary (purchases) ledger of A Austin for January 2004, balancing them at the end of the month

(b)   prepare a purchases ledger control account for January 2004, balancing it at the end of the month

(c)   reconcile the control account balance with the subsidiary accounts at 1 January and 31 January 2004

Note: VAT is to be ignored on all transactions and day books are not required.

11.4   The purchases ledger of Rowcester Traders contains the following accounts on 1 February 2004:

Arley Supplies Limited, balance £1,549.81 credit

Balfour Brothers, balance £39.20 debit

W James & Company, balance £598.27 credit

Mereford Manufacturing Company, balance £495.83 credit

Northern Equipment Limited, balance £727.86 credit

W Williams, balance £1,040.40 credit

The following transactions took place during February:

3 Feb   Bought goods on credit from Arley Supplies Limited, £986.28, and from Balfour Brothers £1,167.24

6 Feb   Paid W Williams a cheque for the balance of the account after deducting 2.5% settlement discount

10 Feb   Bought goods on credit from W James & Company £452.13, and from W Williams £1,595.26

11 Feb   Paid Northern Equipment Limited a cheque for the balance of the account

16 Feb   Returned goods to Arley Supplies Limited for £236.09

17 Feb   Paid Arley Supplies a cheque for the balance of the account, after deducting 2.5% settlement discount

18 Feb   Returned goods to Northern Equipment Limited for £97.39

24 Feb   Paid W James & Company the amount owing by cheque, after deducting 2.5% settlement discount

26 Feb   Bought goods on credit from Arley Supplies Limited £699.84

29 Feb   Transfer of debit balance of £364.68 in the sales ledger to Mereford Manufacturing Company's account in the purchases ledger

You are to:

(a)   write up the accounts in the subsidiary (purchases) ledger of Rowcester Traders for February 2004, balancing them at the end of the month

(b)   prepare a purchases ledger control account for February 2004, balancing it at the end of the month

(c)   reconcile the control account balance with the subsidiary accounts at 1 February and 29 February 2004

Note: VAT is to be ignored on all transactions and day books are not required.

11.5   Prepare purchases ledger control and sales ledger control accounts for the month-ended 31 January 2004 from the following information:

Balances at 1 January 2004

*   debtors, £35,563 debit

*   creditors, £24,080 credit

Totals for the month from the day books

*   sales day book, £205,610

*   purchases day book, £137,825

*   sales returns day book, £3,081

*   purchases returns day book, £1,843

Totals for the month from the cash book

- settlement discount allowed, £548

- payments received from debtors, £197,045

- settlement discount received, £494

- payments made to creditors, £135,048

- debtors' cheques returned unpaid, £856

Other transactions

- set-off entries between sales ledger and purchases ledger, £812

- bad debts written off, £110

- increase in provision for doubtful debts, £250

11.6   You are an accounts assistant at Martinez and Company, a business which imports children's toys and sells them to retailers. The accounts supervisor asks you to review the closing stock of goods for resale at 30 April 2004 (the end of the company's financial year).

The computerised stock records show a stock valuation at cost of £83,290. This figure has been debited to stock control account by the computer and posted to the trading and profit and loss account for the year. However, some stock items have been reduced in price at the year end. The details are shown below:

Stock code	Quantity in stock 30 April 2004	Cost £	Normal selling price £	Reduced selling price £
DC 57	100	5.00	9.00	4.00
JC 55	75	24.00	33.50	22.00
AC 28	220	12.00	19.50	14.00

You are to:

(a)   calculate the adjustments to be made to the stock valuation at 30 April 2004

(b)   prepare a journal entry for authorisation by the accounts supervisor to adjust the stock valuation

(c)   show how the authorised adjustment will be recorded in stock control account

12 THE JOURNAL AND CORRECTION OF ERRORS

For journal entries involving sales ledger and purchases ledger, it is to be assumed that control accounts are incorporated into the double-entry book-keeping system and that the accounts for debtors and creditors are kept in subsidiary ledgers.

Note: a photocopiable blank journal page is printed in the Appendix.

12.1 Which one of the following will not be recorded in the journal?

   (a)   opening transaction of a new business

   (b)   goods taken by the owner for her own use

   (c)   closing stock valuation at the year end

   (d)   petty cash payment for office window cleaning

   Answer (a) or (b) or (c) or (d)

12.2 The purchase of stationery, £25, has been debited in error to office equipment account. Which one of the following journal entries will correct the error?

	Debit		Credit	
(a)	Office equipment	£25	Stationery	£25
(b)	Suspense	£25	Office equipment	£25
(c)	Stationery	£25	Office equipment	£25
(d)	Stationery	£25	Suspense	£25

   Note: VAT is to be ignored

   Answer (a) or (b) or (c) or (d)

12.3 A trial balance fails to agree by £27 and the difference is placed to a suspense account. Later it is found that a payment for postages of £63 has been entered in the accounts as £36. Which one of the following journal entries will correct the error?

	Debit		Credit	
(a)	Suspense	£36	Postages	£36
	Postages	£63	Suspense	£63
(b)	Suspense	£27	Postages	£27
(c)	Postages	£27	Bank	£27
(d)	Postages	£36	Suspense	£36
	Suspense	£63	Postages	£63

   Answer (a) or (b) or (c) or (d)

12.4 What is the effect on the previously-calculated profit and the balance sheet of each of the following?

(a)   sales account has been overcast by £1,000

(b)   closing stock has been undervalued by £250

(c)   telephone expenses account has been undercast by £100

(d)   discount received of £135 has been omitted

(e)   depreciation of the vehicles of £1,250 for the year has not been made

(f)   a reduction of £100 in provision for bad debts has not been made

(g)   bad debts totalling £75 have not been written off

12.5 You have recently taken over writing up the double-entry accounts of Manston Sales Limited. You have found a number of errors made by the previous book-keeper as follows:

(a)   credit sale of goods for £250 to Didsbury Limited has not been entered in the accounts

(b)   a cheque for £195 paid to William Thomas, a creditor, has been debited to the account of another creditor, Thomas Williams

(c)   office stationery costing £50 has been debited to office equipment account

(d)   a credit purchase of goods for £167 from A Carver has been entered in the accounts as £176

(e)   purchases returns account has been undercast by £100 as has electricity account

You are to take each error in turn and:

•   state the type of error

•   show the correcting journal entry

Note: VAT is to be ignored.

12.6 Dave James is the book-keeper for Western Traders Limited. At 30 June 2005 he is unable to balance the trial balance. The difference, £86 credit, is placed to a suspense account in the main ledger pending further investigation.

The following errors are later found:

(a) sales account is overcast by £100

(b) a payment cheque for postages, £65, has been recorded in postages account as £56

(c) commission received of £150 has been debited to both the commission received account and the bank account

(d) stationery expenses of £105, paid by cheque, have not been entered in the expenses account

You are to:

• make journal entries to correct the errors

• show the suspense account after the errors have been corrected

Note: VAT is to be ignored

12.7 Show the journal entries for the following transfers which relate to Jim Hoddle's business for the year ended 30 June 2005:

(a) the balance of sales account, £125,000, is to be transferred to trading and profit and loss account

(b) the balance of purchases account, £78,500, is to be transferred to trading and profit and loss account

(c) closing stock is to be recorded in the accounts at a valuation of £15,500

(d) postages account has a balance of £1,800, but the franking machine meter shows that there is £200 unused; the amount due for the year is to be transferred to profit and loss account

(e) salaries and wages account has a balance of £45,500, but £1,500 is owing; the amount due for the year is to be transferred to profit and loss account

(f) depreciation on vehicles for the year is calculated at £3,000

(g) bad debts written off account has a balance of £180; the amount is to be transferred to profit and loss account

(h) the provision for doubtful debts is £250; the amount is to be increased to £300

13 INCOMPLETE RECORDS

13.1 James Hendry owns a business which sells office stationery. Most of his customers are firms in the area, to whom he sells on credit terms. Although he does not keep a full set of accounting records, the following information is available in respect of the year ended 31 December 2005:

Summary of assets and liabilities:

	1 Jan 2005	31 Dec 2005
	£	£
Shop fittings (cost £10,000)	8,000	7,000
Stock	25,600	29,800
Bank balance	4,000	8,000
Cash	1,000	1,600
Debtors	29,200	20,400
Creditors	20,800	16,000
Accrual: business expenses	–	500

Summary of the business bank account for the year ended 31 December 2005:

	£
Receipts from customers	127,800
Payments to suppliers	82,600
Drawings	20,000
Business expenses	20,600

Other information

Shop fittings are being depreciated at 10% per year, using the straight-line method.

You are to:

(a)   calculate the amount of sales during the year

(b)   calculate the amount of purchases during the year

(c)   calculate the figure for business expenses to be shown in the profit and loss account for the year ended 31 December 2005

(d)   prepare James Hendry's trading and profit and loss account for the year ended 31 December 2005

(e)   prepare James Hendry's balance sheet as at 31 December 2005

Note: VAT is to be ignored on all transactions

13.2 You are preparing the 2004 accounts of Heidi Johnson, who runs a mobile carpet and curtain cleaning business. Heidi keeps few accounting records, but the person who prepared the accounts last year has left a set of working accounts with start of year balances. The balances have been entered in the accounts.

From Heidi's business bank statements you have prepared the following summary for the year ended 31 December 2004:

	£	£
Opening balance		1,547
Receipts:		
Cash takings	2,150	
Receipts from debtors	55,290	
Inheritance	12,000	69,440
		70,987
Payments:		
Payments to creditors	18,450	
Drawings	20,000	
Vehicle expenses	4,250	
General expenses	4,100	
Assistant's wages	9,200	
Purchase of new van on 1 July 2004	13,500	69,500
Closing balance		1,487

The following information is available:

- At 31 December 2004, vehicle expenses were prepaid by £210.
- At 31 December 2004, assistant's wages of £480 were owing.
- At 31 December 2004, debtors were £6,410; creditors were £2,890.
- Invoices to customers during the year totalled £61,450.
- Heidi thinks that debtors amounting to £460 will not pay, and should be written off as bad debts.
- Some customers pay by cheque, while others pay in cash. Heidi has kept no records of the cash received but knows that she paid general expenses of £220 in cash; the rest she kept as drawings. At 31 December 2004, she had a cash float of £125.
- The inheritance was received from the estate of her grandmother: the amount was paid into the business bank account to help finance the new van. (She will keep her old van in order to provide flexibility when she and her assistant are working on different sites.)
- Heidi depreciates vans, using the straight-line method, on the basis of a five-year life from the date of acquisition, with a nil residual value.
- At 31 December 2004 there was a stock of cleaning materials valued at £1,430.

You are to reconstruct the ledger accounts for the year ended 31 December 2004, showing the balances carried forward at the end of the year and/or the amounts to be transferred to profit and loss account. Ledger accounts with appropriate balances are set out on pages 56 to 61.

Notes:
- dates are not required
- the following accounts are not supplied and do not need to be shown:
    - profit and loss
    - sales
    - purchases
    - capital
- VAT is to be ignored on all transactions

Dr   **Bank Account**   Cr

Details	Amount	Details	Amount
	£		£
Balance b/d	1,547		

Dr   **Cash Account**   Cr

Details	Amount	Details	Amount
	£		£
Balance b/d	86		

Dr   **Vehicle Expenses Account**   **Cr**

Details	Amount	Details	Amount
	£	Balance b/d	£ 105

Dr   **Prepayments Account**   **Cr**

Details	Amount	Details	Amount
	£		£

Dr   **Van Account**   **Cr**

Details	Amount	Details	Amount
Balance b/d	£ 10,000		£

Dr　　　　　　　　　　　　　**Depreciation Account**　　　　　　　　　　　　Cr

Details	Amount	Details	Amount
	£		£

Dr　　　　　　**Provision for Depreciation Account – Vans**　　　　　　Cr

Details	Amount	Details	Amount
	£	Balance b/d	£ 6,000

Dr　　　　　　　　　　　　**General Expenses Account**　　　　　　　　　　Cr

Details	Amount	Details	Amount
Balance b/d	£ 110		£

Dr   **Assistant's Wages Account**   **Cr**

Details	Amount	Details	Amount
	£		£

Dr   **Accruals Account**   **Cr**

Details	Amount	Details	Amount
	£		£

Dr   **Debtor's Account**   **Cr**

Details	Amount	Details	Amount
	£		£
Balance b/d	4,120		

Dr		Creditor's Account	Cr
Details	Amount	Details	Amount
	£	Balance b/d	£ 2,250

Dr		Drawings Account	Cr
Details	Amount	Details	Amount
	£		£

Dr		Materials Used Account	Cr
Details	Amount	Details	Amount
Balance b/d (opening stock)	£ 1,050		£

Dr		**Bad Debts Written Off Account**		Cr
Details	Amount	Details		Amount
	£			£

13.3 The following figures are extracted from the accounts of Wyvern Systems Limited for the year ended 30 June 2005:

- sales for the year, £300,000

- opening stock, £20,000

- closing stock, £40,000

- purchases for the year, £260,000

You are to calculate:

(a) cost of sales for the year

(b) gross profit for the year

(c) gross profit percentage mark up

(d) gross profit percentage margin

13.4 Talib Zabbar owns a shop selling children's clothes. He is convinced that one of his employees is stealing goods from the shop. He asks you to calculate from the accounting records the value of stock stolen.

The following information is available:

- sales for the year, £160,000

- opening stock at the beginning of the year, £30,500

- purchases for the year, £89,500

- closing stock at the end of the year, £21,500

- the gross profit margin achieved on all sales is 40 per cent

You are to calculate the value of stock stolen (if any) during the year.

14 PARTNERSHIP FINAL ACCOUNTS

14.1 A partnership may choose to over-ride some or all of the accounting rules in the Partnership Act 1890 by the partners entering into a separate:

(a)   appropriation account

(b)   accounting policy

(c)   partnership agreement

(d)   loan agreement

Answer (a) or (b) or (c) or (d)

14.2 Profits of a two-person partnership are £32,800 before the following are taken into account:

- interest on partners' capital accounts, £1,800
- salary of one partner, £10,000

If the remaining profits are shared equally, how much will each partner receive?

(a)   £10,500

(b)   £11,400

(c)   £12,300

(d)   £16,400

Answer (a) or (b) or (c) or (d)

14.3 Mike and Bernie are in partnership as 'M & B Builders'. The following figures are extracted from their accounts for the year ended 31 December 2004:

		£	
Capital accounts at 1 January 2004:			
	Mike	30,000	Cr
	Bernie	20,000	Cr
Current accounts at 1 January 2004:			
	Mike	1,560	Cr
	Bernie	420	Dr
Drawings for the year:			
	Mike	21,750	
	Bernie	17,350	
Partnership salary:			
	Bernie	7,500	
Interest on capital for the year:			
	Mike	1,500	
	Bernie	1,000	
Share of profits for the year:			
	Mike	20,200	
	Bernie	10,100	

You are to show the partners' capital and current accounts for the year ended 31 December 2004.

14.4   Clark and Pearce are in partnership selling business computer systems. The following trial balance has been taken from their accounts for the year ended 30 June 2004, after the calculation of gross profit:

	Dr £	Cr £
Gross profit		105,000
Salaries	30,400	
Electricity	2,420	
Telephone	3,110	
Rent and rates	10,000	
Discount allowed	140	
Office expenses	10,610	
*Closing stock	41,570	
Debtors and creditors	20,000	6,950
Value Added Tax		5,240
Bad debts written off	1,200	
Provision for doubtful debts		780
Office equipment at cost	52,000	
Provision for depreciation on office equipment		20,800
Clark: Capital account		60,000
Current account		430
Drawings	20,600	
Pearce: Capital account		30,000
Current account		300
Drawings	15,700	
Bank	21,750	
	229,500	229,500

*   Only the closing stock is included in the trial balance because gross profit for the year has been calculated already.

Notes at 30 June 2004:

- depreciate the office equipment at 20 per cent, using the straight-line method
- Pearce is to receive a partnership salary of £12,000
- remaining profits and losses are shared as follows: Clark two-thirds, Pearce one-third

You are to:

(a)   prepare the partnership final accounts for the year ended 30 June 2004, using the extended trial balance method

(b)   show the partners' capital and current accounts for the year

(c)   prepare the partnership final accounts for the year ended 30 June 2004 in proper form, using the conventional format

14.5 Sara and Simon Penny are in partnership running a catering service called 'Class Caterers'. The following trial balance has been taken from their accounts for the year ended 31 March 2005:

	Dr £	Cr £
Capital accounts:		
Sara		10,000
Simon		6,000
Current accounts:		
Sara		560
Simon		1,050
Drawings:		
Sara	12,700	
Simon	7,400	
Purchases	11,300	
Sales		44,080
Opening stock	2,850	
Wages	8,020	
Rent and rates	4,090	
Sundry expenses	1,390	
Equipment	8,000	
Debtors	4,500	
Creditors		5,850
Value Added Tax		1,350
Bank	8,640	
	68,890	68,890

Notes at 31 March 2005:

- stock was valued at £3,460
- sundry expenses owing, £110
- depreciation is to be charged on the equipment at 10 per cent per year
- Sara is to receive a partnership salary of £8,000
- interest is to be allowed on partners' capital accounts at 10 per cent per year
- remaining profits and losses are to be shared equally

You are to:

(a) prepare the partnership final accounts for the year ended 31 March 2005, using the extended trial balance method

(b) show the partners' capital and current accounts for the year

(c) prepare the partnership final accounts for the year ended 31 March 2005 in proper form, using the conventional format

14.6   Anne Adams and Jenny Beeson are partners in an electrical supplies shop called 'A & B Electrics'. The following trial balance has been taken from their accounts for the year ended 30 June 2005:

		Dr £	Cr £
Capital accounts:	A Adams		30,000
	J Beeson		20,000
Current accounts:	A Adams		780
	J Beeson		920
Drawings:	A Adams	16,000	
	J Beeson	10,000	
Opening stock		26,550	
Purchases and sales		175,290	250,140
Returns		1,360	850
Rent and rates		8,420	
Wages		28,700	
Motor vehicle expenses		2,470	
General expenses		6,210	
Motor vehicle at cost		12,000	
Fixtures and fittings at cost		4,000	
Provision for depreciation:	motor vehicle		3,000
	fixtures and fittings		800
Debtors and creditors		6,850	12,360
Value Added Tax			2,410
Bank		22,009	
Cash		1,376	
Bad debts written off		175	
Provision for doubtful debts			150
		321,410	321,410

Notes at 30 June 2005:
- stock is valued at £27,750
- rates paid in advance £250
- wages owing £320
- provision for doubtful debts to be equal to 2 per cent debtors
- depreciation on fixtures and fittings to be provided at 10 per cent per year using the straight line method
- depreciation on motor vehicles to be provided at 25 per cent per year using the reducing balance method
- Anne Adams is to receive a partnership salary of £6,000
- remaining profits and losses are to be shared equally

You are to:

(a)   prepare the partnership final accounts for the year ended 30 June 2005, using the extended trial balance method

(b)   show the partners' capital and current accounts for the year

(c)   prepare the partnership final accounts for the year ended 30 June 2005 in proper form, using the conventional format

15 CHANGES IN PARTNERSHIPS

15.1 Mia, Nell and Olly are in partnership sharing profits equally. Mia is to retire and it is agreed that goodwill is worth £30,000. After Mia's retirement, Nell and Olly will continue to run the partnership and will share profits equally. What will be the goodwill adjustments to Nell's capital account?

(a)   debit £10,000,   credit £10,000

(b)   debit £10,000,   credit £15,000

(c)   debit £15,000,   credit £15,000

(d)   debit £15,000,   credit £10,000

Answer (a) or (b) or (c) or (d)

15.2 Norman and Oliver are in partnership sharing profits equally. Each has a capital account with a balance of £75,000. Peter joins as a new partner introducing £80,000 capital. The new profit share will be Norman (2), Oliver (2) and Peter (1). An adjustment is made for goodwill on the admission of Peter to the value of £40,000, but no goodwill is to be left in the accounts. What will be the balance of Oliver's capital account after the creation and write off of goodwill?

(a)   £71,000

(b)   £79,000

(c)   £91,000

(d)   £95,000

Answer (a) or (b) or (c) or (d)

15.3 The partnership of Fame, Fortune and Fear has asked you to assist its book-keeper in the finalisation of its accounts for the year ended 31 March 2005.

The following information is available:

* The net profit of the business for the year is £152,000, before taking into account any appropriations.

* The original partners of the business are Fame and Fortune. They shared profits on an equal basis until 1 April 2004 when Fear then joined them. Fear agreed to introduce £60,000 by cheque on admission to the business. It was then agreed that the new profit sharing ratio would be:

Fame	3/8
Fortune	3/8
Fear	2/8

- On 1 April 2004 goodwill was valued at £80,000. No adjustment was made for goodwill at that time, but it is now the wish of the partners that goodwill is introduced against their opening capital accounts. (No goodwill account is to be maintained in the accounts of the partnership).

- Partnership salaries for the year to 31 March 2005 are as follows:

	£
Fame	20,000
Fortune	20,000
Fear	30,000

- All partners receive interest of 10 per cent per annum on the year end balance of their capital accounts.

- The credit balances on capital and current accounts as at 1 April 2004 were as follows:

	Capital Accounts	Current Accounts
	£	£
Fame	110,000	6,500
Fortune	90,000	7,800

- Partners' drawings were as follows:

	£
Fame	28,000
Fortune	32,000
Fear	36,000

Task 1

Prepare the partners' capital accounts for the year ended 31 March 2005, recording all the necessary entries for the admission of Fear to the partnership.

Task 2

Prepare the partnership appropriation account for the year ended 31 March 2005.

Task 3

Prepare the partners' current accounts for the year ended 31 March 2005.

15.4 Henry, Ian and Jenny are in partnership sharing profits equally. Ian retired on 31 December 2004. The balance sheet drawn up immediately before Ian's retirement was as follows:

	£	£
Fixed assets		120,000
Current assets		55,000
Bank		15,000
		190,000
Current liabilities		50,000
		140,000
Capital Accounts:		
Henry	42,000	
Ian	43,000	
Jenny	50,000	
		135,000
Current Accounts:		
Henry	4,000	
Ian	(2,000)	
Jenny	3,000	
		5,000
		140,000

Upon Ian's retirement from the partnership:

- goodwill was agreed to be worth £36,000
- his current account balance was to be transferred to his capital account
- he was to be paid £10,000 of his capital and share of the goodwill by cheque, and the balance was to be left as a loan to the partnership
- Henry and Jenny were to continue in partnership sharing profits and losses equally
- No goodwill is to remain in the accounts

Task 1

You are to prepare the partners' capital accounts, showing the retirement of Ian.

Task 2

You are to show the balance sheet immediately after Ian's retirement from the partnership.

15.5   Nisha and Dil are in partnership. Net profit for the year ended 30 June 2005 is £36,400 before appropriation of profit. Their capital account balances at 30 June 2005 are Nisha £25,000, Dil £20,000. Their partnership agreement allows for the following:

- partnership salaries

  - Nisha £8,000

  - Dil   £12,000

- interest is allowed on capital at 4 per cent per year on the balance at the year end

- profit share, effective until 31 December 2004

  - Nisha 50%

  - Dil   50%

- profit share, effective from 1 January 2005

  - Nisha 60%

  - Dil   40%

Notes:

- no accounting entries for goodwill are to be recorded

- profits accrued evenly during the year

- drawings for the year were: Nisha £15,200, Dil £22,100

Task 1

Prepare the appropriation account for the partnership of Nisha and Dil for the year ended 30 June 2005.

Task 2

Update the current accounts for the partnership for the year ended 30 June 2005. Show clearly the balances carried down.

Dr				**Partners' Current Accounts**			Cr
2004/05		Nisha	Dil	2004/05		Nisha	Dil
		£	£			£	£
1 Jul	Balance b/d	650	–	1 Jul	Balance b/d	–	1,950

Practice Examination 1
Sarah Glass; KW Enterprise

NVQ Element coverage

5.1 maintaining records relating to capital acquisition and disposal

5.2 collecting and collating information for the preparation of final accounts

5.3 preparing the final accounts of sole traders and partnerships

Suggested time allocation

Three hours and fifteen minutes (to include a recommended fifteen minutes reading time).

PRACTICE EXAMINATION 1
SARAH GLASS; KW ENTERPRISE

This Examination is in two sections.

You have to show competence in both sections.

You should therefore attempt and aim to complete every task in both sections.

You should spend about 80 minutes on Section 1 and 100 minutes on Section 2.

SECTION 1

You should spend about 80 minutes on this section.

DATA

Sarah Glass is considering buying a small wholesale business from Hassan Abdul.

Hassan Abdul has provided some financial information for his business, which is set out below and on the next page.

You are an accounting technician at Aggie Accountancy, an accounting firm which is advising Sarah Glass.

Assets and liabilities as at 30 April 2003

	£
Freehold premises at cost	104,000
Less Depreciation to date	20,800
	83,200
Fixtures and fittings at cost	22,750
Less Depreciation to date	13,650
	9,100
Stock	43,160
Debtors	52,300
Prepaid general expenses	700
Cash	1,000
	97,160
Creditors	46,750
Bank overdraft	22,600
	69,350

Summary of the business bank account for the year ended 30 April 2004

2004	£	2004	£
Cash sales	292,180	Opening balance	22,600
Receipts from debtors	722,800	Payments to creditors	789,950
		General expenses	8,110
		Salaries	92,420
		Drawings	36,800
		Closing balance	65,100
	1,014,980		1,014,980

Other information

- The profit margin achieved on all sales was 20%

- The value of the closing stock held on 30 April 2004 is unknown

- Depreciation is calculated as follows:

    Premises – 2% per annum on cost

    Fixtures and fittings – 10% per annum on cost

- All cash is banked at the end of each day, apart from a cash float. During the year, the cash float was decreased from £1,000 to £800

- On 30 April 2004 the outstanding balances were:

	£
Creditors	64,100
Debtors	59,020
Accrual for general expenses	210

Sarah Glass has asked you to calculate some key figures for the year ended 30 April 2004.

Task 1.1

Calculate the total value of the credit sales for the year ended 30 April 2004.

Task 1.2

Calculate the total sales for the year ended 30 April 2004.

Task 1.3

Calculate the total value of the purchases for the year ended 30 April 2004.

Task 1.4

Calculate the value of the closing stock held on 30 April 2004.

Task 1.5

Starting with the gross profit for the year ended 30 April 2004 (calculated in 1.4 above), prepare the profit and loss account for the year ended 30 April 2004. Show clearly the net profit or loss for the year.

Task 1.6

Show the net book value of the fixed assets held on 30 April 2004.

Task 1.7

When Sarah Glass looks at your figures, she does not understand why the closing balance in the bank account is different to the net profit shown in task 1.5.

(a)   Give TWO examples of transactions that affect the profit figure, but do not affect the bank account.

(b)   Give ONE example of a transaction that affects the bank account, but does not directly affect the profit figure

DATA

Sarah Glass is considering forming a partnership with her brother who could provide some of the money needed to fund the purchase of the business from Hassan Abdul.

Sarah Glass does not understand how partnerships are shown in accounts. She is worried that the money each partner puts into, and takes out of, the business, will not be shown separately.

Task 1.8

Using the headed paper on the next page, write a memo to Sarah Glass explaining:

*   how partner interests are shown in the financial statements of a partnership
*   the difference between the types of accounts that exist
*   what types of transactions the different accounts would show

MEMO
To: Sarah Glass   **From:**   Accounting Technician   **Subject:** Partnership accounts   **Date:**   Today

SECTION 2

You should spend about 100 minutes on this section.

DATA

Kelly Wainwright is the proprietor of KW Enterprise, a business that buys and sells carpets and other floor coverings.

*   The financial year end is 30 June 2004.

*   You are employed by Kelly Wainwright to assist with the bookkeeping.

*   The business currently operates a manual system consisting of a main (general) ledger, a subsidiary (sales) ledger and a subsidiary (purchases) ledger.

*   Double entry takes place in the main (general) ledger. Individual accounts of debtors and creditors are kept in subsidiary accounts.

*   You use a purchases day book, a sales day book, a purchases returns day book and a sales returns day book. Totals from the various columns of the day books are transferred into the main (general) ledger.

At the end of the financial year on 30 June 2004, the balances were extracted from the main (general) ledger and entered in an extended trial balance as shown on the next page.

It was found that the total of the debit column of the trial balance did not agree with the total of the credit column. The difference was posted to a suspense account.

Task 2.1

Make appropriate entries in the adjustment columns of the extended trial balance on the next page to take account of the following.

(a)   Depreciation needs to be provided as follows:

*   Motor vehicles – 25% per annum reducing balance method

*   Fixtures and fittings – 15% per annum straight line method

(b)   Rent payable is £3,000 per month.

(c)   An invoice relating to goods received by KW Enterprise on 29 June 2004 had not been entered in the accounts. The invoice totalled £2,350 including VAT at 17.5%. The goods have been included in the stock valuation on 30 June 2004.

(d)   Stock was valued at cost on 30 June 2004 at £30,040. This includes £625 which is the cost of a carpet that is dirty and needs cleaning. The cost of cleaning it will be £50, and the carpet can then be sold for £300.

(e)   On reviewing the debtors, Kelly Wainwright decides that £300 should be written off. The provision for doubtful debts should be 4% of the outstanding debtors.

KW Enterprise

Trial balance as at 30 June 2004

Description	Ledger balance		Adjustments	
	Dr £	Cr £	Dr £	Cr £
Capital		61,280		
Sales		487,360		
Sales returns	8,900			
Purchases	286,330			
Purchases returns		650		
Stock at 1 July 2003	25,870			
Rent	33,000			
General expenses	87,700			
Motor expenses	28,540			
Bad debts	1,220			
Provision for doubtful debts		3,200		
Motor vehicles (M.V.) at cost	36,000			
Provision for depreciation (M.V.)		19,560		
Fixtures and fittings (F&F) at cost	57,020			
Provision for depreciation (F&F)		34,580		
Drawings	30,000			
Sales ledger control account	56,550			
Purchases ledger control account		31,500		
Bank		2,700		
VAT		10,070		
Suspense		230		
Depreciation				
Provision for doubtful debts – adjustment				
Closing stock – P & L				
Closing stock – balance sheet				
Accruals				
Totals	**651,130**	**651,130**		

DATA

You have found the following errors.

(a)   The VAT column of the sales day book had been undercast by £380.

(b)   The net column of the sales day book had been overcast by £870.

(c)   Sales of £5,080 had been transferred from the total column of the sales day book into the sales ledger control account as £5,800.

Task 2.2

Prepare journal entries to correct the errors using the blank journal below.

Dates and narratives are not required.

Note: Do not adjust your answer to task 2.1 (e).

Journal		
	Dr	Cr
	£	£

DATA

On 30 June 2004 the balances of the accounts in the subsidiary (purchases) ledger were listed, totalled and compared with the updated balance in the purchases ledger control account.

The list of balances totalled £33,770. After an investigation, the following errors were found in the list taken from the subsidiary (purchases) ledger.

(a)   A creditor account with a balance of £290 had been omitted from the list.

(b)   A credit purchase of £960 (inclusive of VAT) had been omitted from a creditor's account.

(c)   Purchase returns of £80 (inclusive of VAT) had been omitted from a creditor's account.

(d)   A payment to a creditor of £500 had been credited to the creditor's account.

(e)   A creditor's balance of £780 had been entered in the list as £870.

Task 2.3

Enter the appropriate adjustments in the table below. For each adjustment show clearly the amount involved and whether the amount is to be added or subtracted.

		£
Total from purchase ledger		....
Adjustment for (a)	add / subtract	....
Adjustment for (b)	add / subtract	....
Adjustment for (c)	add / subtract	....
Adjustment for (d)	add / subtract	....
Adjustment for (e)	add / subtract	....
Revised total to agree with purchases ledger control account		....

Task 2.4

Some of the fixtures and fittings used by KW Enterprise were originally purchased on 1 January 2003 for £8,400. Assume these fixtures and fittings were sold on 1 August 2004 for £6,000.

(a)   What would be the net book value of these fixtures and fittings on the date of disposal if the depreciation is calculated on a monthly basis?

£ . . . .

. . . .

(b)   What would be the amount of profit or loss on disposal of the fixtures and fittings?

(Circle the correct answer for profit or loss)

Profit / Loss

£ . . . .

. . . .

Task 2.5

The list of balances on page 209 includes an amount of £10,070 as VAT.

(a)   To whom will KW Enterprise pay this amount?

(b)   Explain how the VAT balance has been arrived at.

DATA

- Kelly Wainwright has looked at the work you have done so far on the accounts.

- She is interested in the reconciliation you did between the subsidiary (purchases) ledger and the purchases ledger control account.

- She does not understand why you did the reconciliation.

Task 2.6

Using the headed paper on the next page, write a brief memo to Kelly Wainwright, explaining:

- the purpose of the subsidiary (purchases) ledger

- whether the subsidiary (purchases) ledger is part of the double-entry accounting system

- the purpose of the purchases ledger control account

- whether the purchases ledger control account is part of the double-entry accounting system

- the reasons for doing the reconciliation

MEMO

To:	Kelly Wainwright
From:	Accounting Technician
Subject:	Reconciliations
Date:	Today

Practice Examination 2
David Nix; ABC Traders

NVQ Element coverage

5.1 maintaining records relating to capital acquisition and disposal

5.2 collecting and collating information for the preparation of final accounts

5.3 preparing the final accounts of sole traders and partnerships

Suggested time allocation

Three hours and fifteen minutes (to include a recommended fifteen minutes reading time).

PRACTICE EXAMINATION 2
DAVID NIX; ABC TRADERS

This Examination is in two sections.

You have to show competence in both sections.

You should therefore attempt and aim to complete every task in both sections.

You should spend about 80 minutes on section 1, and 100 minutes on section 2.

SECTION 1

You should spend about 80 minutes on this section.

DATA

David Nix started trading on 1 June 2003. He opened a shop selling general groceries.

David Nix does not keep a double-entry book-keeping system.

You are an accounting technician at Aggie Accountancy, an accounting firm which is preparing the final accounts for David Nix. You are working on his accounts for the year ended 31 May 2004. David Nix has given you the following information.

A summary of the business bank account for the year ended 31 May 2004

2004	£	2004	£
From cash account	89,750	Payments to trade creditors	59,400
		Wages	8,105
		General expenses	7,550
		Drawings	11,000
Closing balance	1,305	Fixtures	5,000
	91,055		91,055

Other information

• The cash from sales is banked at the end of the day, except a float of £100 that is kept in the till. During the year, the following cash payments were made from the till, before banking.

	£
General expenses	2,150
Wages	1,900

• The value of the stock on 31 May 2004 was unknown, but the profit margin achieved on all sales was 1/3.

• The fixtures are expected to last for five years, depreciating evenly over time, with no residual value.

• On 31 May 2004, the outstanding balances were:

	£
Trade creditors	9,320
General expenses	780

Task 1.1

Prepare the cash account for the year ended 31 May 2004, clearly showing the total sales.

Task 1.2

Calculate the gross profit for the year ended 31 May 2004.

Task 1.3

Calculate the total purchases for the year ended 31 May 2004.

Task 1.4

Calculate the cost of the closing stock for the year ended 31 May 2004.

ADDITIONAL DATA

David Nix tells you that the value of the closing stock, at cost, on 31 May 2004 was £3,650. Also, in February 2004, the shop was broken into and some stock was stolen. He does not know the value of the stolen stock.

Task 1.5

Calculate the cost of the stolen stock.

Task 1.6

Calculate the actual gross profit for the year ended 31 May 2004.

Task 1.7

Starting with the gross profit for the year ended 31 May 2004 (calculated in 1.6, above), prepare David Nix's profit and loss account for the year ended 31 May 2004. Show clearly his net profit or loss for the year.

Task 1.8

David has heard of a profit mark-up, but does not understand the difference between profit margin and profit mark up.

Explain the difference between profit margin and profit mark-up.

DATA

David Nix needs to buy some more fixtures, but cannot afford to pay for them out of the bank account. He has heard about leasing and hire purchase of fixed assets, and needs to know more about these methods of financing.

Task 1.9

Using the headed paper on the next page, write a memo to David Nix explaining:

- the terms leasing and hire purchase;
- the difference between the two methods of financing.

MEMO
To: David Nix
From: Accounting Technician
Subject: Leasing and hire purchase
Date: Today

SECTION 2

You should spend about 100 minutes on this section.

DATA

Andrea and Brian Colvin are the owners of ABC Traders, a business that buys and sells garden furniture.

*   The financial year end is 30 June 2004.
*   The business uses an integrated computerised accounting system consisting of a main ledger, a purchases ledger and a stock ledger.
*   There are no credit customers.
*   You work for Aggie Accountancy, an accounting firm which prepares final accounts for Andrea and Brian Colvin.

At the end of the financial year on 30 June 2004, the trial balance shown on the next page was taken from the computer system.

	Dr £	Cr £
Accruals		5,500
Advertising	8,740	
Bank	51,809	
Capital account – Andrea		35,000
Capital account – Brian		40,000
Cash in hand	550	
Closing stock – trading account		58,450
Closing stock – balance sheet	58,450	
Computer equipment at cost	12,900	
Computer equipment accumulated depreciation		7,460
Current account – Andrea		9,045
Current account – Brian	3,750	
Drawings – Andrea	25,240	
Drawings – Brian	19,610	
Fixtures and fittings at cost	48,140	
Fixtures and fittings accumulated depreciation		17,890
General expenses	82,440	
Opening stock	69,375	
Prepayments	3,500	
Purchases	476,725	
Purchases ledger control		45,320
Rent	18,200	
Sales		762,918
VAT		13,500
Wages	115,654	
Total	995,083	995,083

DATA

After checking the trial balance, you discover

*   some year-end adjustments that need to be made
*   some errors that need correcting

(a)   Depreciation needs to be provided as follows:

*   fixtures and fittings – 10% per annum straight line method
*   computer equipment – 25% per annum reducing balance method

(b)   General expenses include insurance of £2,400, which was paid for the year ending 31 December 2004.

(c)   £2,000 is owed in wages on 30 June 2004.

(d)   An invoice of £1,250 for advertising has been debited to purchases account.

(e)   A journal entry for general expenses accrued of £400 relating to June 2004 has been entered into the accounting system as:

Debit   Accruals   £400

Credit General expenses   £400

(f)   The closing stock valuation in the trial balance is taken from the computerised accounting system at cost price. Some items were reduced in price after the financial year end. The details are as follows:

Stock code	Quantity in stock 30 June 2004	Cost £	Normal selling price £	Reduced selling price £
FRO	50	25.00	45.00	30.00
TKT	20	80.00	150.00	75.00
WHE	12	20.00	30.00	10.00

Task 2.1

Prepare journal entries to record the above adjustments and correct the errors.

Dates and narratives are not required. Use the blank journal provided on the next page. There is space for your workings below the journal.

JOURNAL		
	Dr £	Cr £

Workings

Task 2.2

Prepare a profit and loss account for the partnership for the year ended 30 June 2004, showing clearly the gross profit and the net profit. Use the trial balance from page 93 and your journal adjustments from page 95.

ADDITIONAL DATA

The partnership agreement allows for the following:

Partners' salaries

- Andrea   £12,000
- Brian   £10,000

Interest on capital

5% per annum on the balance at the year end

Profit share

- Andrea   one-half
- Brian   one-half

Task 2.3

Prepare the appropriation account for the partnership for the year ended 30 June 2004.

Task 2.4

Update the current accounts for the partnership for the year ended 30 June 2004. Show clearly the balances carried down.

CURRENT ACCOUNTS

		Andrea	Brian			Andrea	Brian
2003		£	£	2003		£	£
1 Jul	Balance b/d		3,750	1 Jul	Balance b/d	9,045	

Task 2.5

Prepare a balance sheet for the partnership as at 30 June 2004, showing clearly the total net assets. Use the trial balance from page 93 and your journal adjustments from page 95.

ADDITIONAL DATA

From 1 July 2004, the partners agree to change the profit share to

- Andrea   two-thirds
- Brian   one-third

It is agreed that goodwill should be valued at £30,000. No goodwill is to remain in the accounts following the change.

Task 2.6

(a)   Update the capital accounts for the partnership as at 1 July 2004 in order to reflect the change in profit share. Show clearly the balances carried down.

CAPITAL ACCOUNTS

		Andrea £	Brian £			Andrea £	Brian £
2004				2004			
				1 Jul	Balances b/d	35,000	40,000

(b)   On reviewing her capital account following changes to the profit share, Andrea wants to know why her capital account balance has altered.

Draft a brief note to Andrea Colvin explaining

- why the adjustment to her capital account was necessary
- how the adjustment has affected her capital in the business

Note to Andrea Colvin

Practice Examination 3
Fresh Produce; Cookequip

(AAT sample material) © AAT, 2003

NVQ Element coverage

5.1 maintaining records relating to capital acquisition and disposal

5.2 collecting and collating information for the preparation of final accounts

5.3 preparing the final accounts of sole traders and partnerships

Suggested time allocation

Three hours and fifteen minutes (to include a recommended fifteen minutes reading time).

PRACTICE EXAMINATION 3
FRESH PRODUCE; COOKEQUIP

This Examination is in two sections.

You have to show competence in both sections.

You should therefore attempt and aim to complete every task in both sections.

You should spend about 80 minutes on Section 1 and 100 minutes on Section 2.

SECTION 1

You should spend about 80 minutes on this section.

DATA

Tony Bond owns Fresh Produce, a business that buys and sells fruit and vegetables. All sales are on credit terms.

Tony Bond does not keep a double entry bookkeeping system.

You are an accounting technician at A1 Accountancy, an accounting firm which prepares the final accounts for Fresh Produce. You are working on the accounts for Fresh Produce for the year ending 31 December 2004. Your colleague has already summarised the cash and bank accounts, which are shown below.

Fresh Produce			
Bank account summary for the year ended 31 December 2004			
	£		£
Receipts from debtors	868,760	Opening balance	9,380
Closing balance	4,985	Purchases	661,300
		Vehicle running expenses	9,065
		Purchase of replacement vehicle	7,500
		Wages	42,500
		Drawings	25,500
		Cash	118,500
	873,745		873,745

Fresh Produce

Cash account summary for the year ended 31 December 2004

	£		£
Opening balance	3,500	Purchases	118,700
Bank	118,500	Closing balance	3,300
	122,000		122,000

The balance sheet from last year is also available:

Fresh Produce

Balance sheet as at 31 December 2003

	£ Cost	£ Accumulated Depreciation	£ Net Book Value
Fixed assets			
Vehicles	23,025	12,750	10,275
Current assets			
Trade debtors		152,360	
Prepayment		1,535	
Cash		3,500	
		157,395	
Current liabilities			
Bank overdraft		9,380	
Net current assets			148,015
Total net assets			158,290
Capital account			158,290

Other information

- Tony Bond gives unsold stock to a charity at the end of each day, so there are no stocks.
- The prepayment was for vehicle insurance.
- The total owed by debtors on 31 December 2004 was £148,600.
- There are no trade creditors.
- During the year Tony Bond part-exchanged one of the vehicles. The vehicle originally cost £8,000 in 2001. He was given a part-exchange allowance of £2,000 against a replacement vehicle.
- The depreciation policy is 25% per annum reducing balance. A full year's depreciation is applied in the year of acquisition and none in the year of disposal.
- Vehicle insurance of £1,200 was paid in October 2004 for the twelve months to September 2005.

Task 1.1

Prepare the sales ledger control account for the year ended 31 December 2004, showing clearly the total sales.

Dr   **Sales Ledger Control Account**   Cr

2004		£	2004		£

Task 1.2

Calculate the total purchases for the year ended 31 December 2004.

Task 1.3

Calculate the net book value of the vehicle that was part-exchanged during the year.

Task 1.4

Prepare the disposals account for the year ending 31 December 2004.

Dr   **Disposals Account**   Cr

2004		£	2004		£

Task 1.5

(a)   Calculate the cost of the replacement vehicle purchased during the year ending 31 December 2004.

(b)   Calculate the revised total vehicle cost as at 31 December 2004.

(c)   Calculate the depreciation charge for the year ending 31 December 2004.

(d)   Calculate the updated accumulated depreciation as at 31 December 2004.

Task 1.6

(a)   Calculate the adjustment necessary as at 31 December 2004 for the vehicle insurance paid in October 2004, stating clearly whether it is a prepayment or an accrual.

(b)   Calculate the adjusted vehicle running expenses for the year ended 31 December 2004.

(c)   Name the accounting concept, referred to in FRS18, which supports the adjustment you have made to vehicle running expenses.

Task 1.7

Prepare a trial balance as at 31 December 2004, taking into account your answers to the above tasks, and all the other information you have been given.

	FRESH PRODUCE	
TRIAL BALANCE AS AT 31 DECEMBER 2004		
	Dr	Cr
Name of account	£	£
....	....	....
....	....	....
....	....	....
....	....	....
....	....	....
....	....	....
....	....	....
....	....	....
....	....	....
....	....	....
....	....	....
....	....	....
....	....	....
....	....	....
....	....	....
Total	....	....

Task 1.8

You see a note in the file stating that Tony Bond normally marks up all his purchases by 15%. Your supervisor suggests that you check your sales figures in Task 1.1 by using this information.

(a)   Using your purchases figure from Task 1.2 and the normal mark-up of 15%, recalculate the sales for the year ending 31 December 2004.

(b)   Calculate the difference between the figure you have calculated in 1.8(a), and your answer to Task 1.1.

(c)   Draft a memo to your supervisor, Maisie Bell. In your memo:

•   state the discrepancy you have found in preparing the sales figure for Fresh Produce, referring to your answer to Task 1.8(b)

•   offer a possible explanation for the discrepancy

•   ask Maisie Bell what she would like you to do about the discrepancy

Use the memo format on the next page.

MEMO		
To:	Maisie Bell	
From:	Accounting Technician	
Subject:	Fresh Produce discrepancy	
Date:	15 January 2005	

SECTION 2

You should spend about 100 minutes on this section.

DATA

David Arthur and Liz Stanton are the owners of Cookequip, a shop selling cookery equipment to the public.

- The financial year end is 31 December 2004.
- The business uses an integrated computerised accounting system consisting of a main ledger, a purchase ledger and a stock ledger.
- There are no credit customers.
- You work for a firm of chartered accountants who prepare final accounts for David Arthur and Liz Stanton.

At the end of the financial year on 31st December 2004, the following trial balance was taken from the computer system:

	Dr £	Cr £
Accruals		5,500
Advertising	10,893	
Bank	11,983	
Capital account – Liz		30,000
Capital account – David		10,000
Cash in hand	500	
Closing stock – trading account		28,491
Closing stock – balance sheet	28,491	
Computer equipment at cost	15,000	
Computer equipment accumulated depreciation		3,750
Consultancy fees	3,800	
Current account – Liz		6,750
Current account – David	3,500	
Drawings – Liz	5,000	
Drawings – David	16,250	
Fixtures and fittings at cost	90,000	
Fixtures and fittings accumulated depreciation		53,000
Office expenses	4,000	
Opening stock	25,834	
Prepayments	5,000	
Purchases	287,532	
Purchases ledger control		14,811
Rent	23,000	
Sales		465,382
VAT control		11,453
Wages	98,354	
Total	629,137	629,137

Task 2.1

After checking the trial balance, you discover

- some year-end adjustments that need to be made

- some errors that need correcting

Prepare journal entries to record the following adjustments and correct the errors. Dates and narratives are not required. Use the blank journal provided on the next page. There is space for your workings below the journal.

(a)   Depreciation needs to be provided as follows:

- Fixtures and fittings – 20% per annum reducing balance method

- Computer equipment – 25% per annum straight line method

(b)   The closing stock valuation in the trial balance is taken from the computerised system at cost, but some items were reduced in price after the year end. The details are shown below:

Stock Code	Quantity in stock 31 December 2004	Cost £	Normal selling price £	Reduced selling price £
AB625	150	7.00	8.00	4.00
AD184	2	180.00	220.00	150.00
BS552	4	6.00	10.25	7.50

(c)   Accountancy fees of £1,500 need to be accrued.

(d)   A journal entry for prepaid rent of £1,500 relating to January 2005 has been posted as follows:

Dr   Rent   £1,500

Cr   Prepayments   £1,500

(e)   An invoice for £500 for consultancy fees has been debited to the purchases account.

JOURNAL		
	Dr £	Cr £

Workings

Task 2.2

Prepare a profit and loss account for the partnership for the year ended 31 December 2004, showing clearly the gross profit and the net profit. Use the trial balance from page 111 and your journal adjustments from page 113.

ADDITIONAL DATA

- The partnership agreement allows for the following:

    Partners' salaries

    - Liz   £8,000
    - David   £12,000

    Interest on capital

    - 2.5% per annum on the balance at the year end

    Profit share, effective until 30 June 2004

    - Liz   two thirds
    - David one third

    Profit share, effective from 1 July 2004

    - Liz   one half
    - David one half

- No accounting entries for goodwill are required.
- Profit accrued evenly during the year

Task 2.3

Prepare the appropriation account for the partnership for the year ended 31 December 2004.

Task 2.4

Update the current accounts for the partnership for the year ended 31 December 2004. Show clearly the balances carried down.

CURRENT ACCOUNTS

2004		Liz £	David £	2004		Liz £	David £
1 Jan	Balance b/d		3,500	1 Jan	Balance b/d	6,750	

Task 2.5

On reviewing the accounts, Liz Stanton asked a question about the partners' current accounts. She wanted to know why the balances brought down for the two partners were on opposite sides.

Draft a note to Liz Stanton explaining:

(a)   what the balance on a partner's current account represents

(b)   what a debit balance on a partner's current account means

(c)   what a credit balance on a partner's current account means

Note to Liz Stanton

DATA

On reviewing the accounts, David Arthur wants to know why you adjusted the stock valuation from the computer system and how this affected the profit you calculated.

Task 2.6

Draft a note to David Arthur explaining:

(a)   why the adjustment was necessary, naming the relevant accounting standard

(b)   how your adjustment affected the profit

Note to David Arthur

Page for workings

Practice examination 4
Jenny Shaw; HJ Cleaning

Element coverage

5.1 maintaining records relating to capital acquisition and disposal

5.2 collecting and collating information for the preparation of final accounts

5.3 preparing the final accounts of sole traders and partnerships

Suggested time allocation

Three hours plus 15 minutes' reading time.

PRACTICE EXAMINATION 4
JENNY SHAW; HJ CLEANING

This Examination is in two sections.

You have to show competence in both sections.

You should therefore attempt and aim to complete every task in both sections.

You should spend about 80 minutes on section 1, and 100 minutes on section 2.

SECTION 1

You should spend about 80 minutes on this section.

DATA

Jenny Shaw started trading on 1 April 2006. She provides a laundry service to hotels. She does not keep a double entry bookkeeping system. She is not registered for Value Added Tax (VAT).

You are an accounting technician at Harper and Co, the accounting firm that Jenny has asked to prepare her first set of final accounts for the year ended 31 March 2007. Jenny has already summarised the bank account, which is shown below.

Jenny Shaw

Bank summary for the year ended 31 March 2007

	£		£
Capital	10,000	Rent of premises	6,975
Receipts from trade debtors	48,500	Payroll expenses	15,000
		Creditors for supplies	2,950
		Travel expenses	2,800
		General expenses	2,050
		Equipment lease payments	1,800
		Drawings	18,000
		Closing balance	8,925
	58,500		58,500

Additional information

- Trade debtors owed £6,500 on 31 March 2007.

- On 31 March 2007, £350 was owed to creditors for supplies.

- Jenny Shaw transferred her own vehicle to the business on 1 April 2006. It was valued at £4,000.

- The vehicle is to be written off over 4 years on a straight line basis with a residual value of £600.

- During March 2007 a payment of £1,395 was made for rent of premises. This was for the period 1 April 2007 to 30 June 2007.

- During April 2007 a payment was made for electricity for £190. This was for electricity used during March 2007. Electricity is charged to general expenses.

Task 1.1

Prepare the sales ledger control account for the year ended 31 March 2007, showing clearly the credit sales.

Sales ledger control account

	£		£

Task 1.2

Prepare the purchases ledger control account for the year ended 31 March 2007, showing clearly the credit purchases of supplies.

Purchases ledger control account

	£		£

Task 1.3

Prepare the capital account for the year ended 31 March 2007.

Capital account

	£		£

Task 1.4

Calculate the depreciation charge for vehicles, for the year ended 31 March 2007.

_____

_____

_____

_____

_____

Task 1.5

Using the accruals concept, calculate the amounts to be charged to the profit and loss account for the year ended 31 March 2007:

(a)   Rent of premises

_____

_____

_____

_____

_____

(b)   General expenses

_____

_____

_____

_____

_____

Task 1.6

Jenny Shaw has just discovered that one of her customers, Prime Hotel Limited, has gone out of business. The company owes her £1,490, which is included in the closing debtors figure on page 121. Jenny knows she will not be able to recover any of the debt. Draft the journal entry required to account for this.

JOURNAL

	Dr £	Cr £

Task 1.7

Complete the trial balance below as at 31 March 2007, taking into account your answers to the above tasks, and all the other information you have been given.

Jenny Shaw
Trial balance as at 31 March 2007

	Dr £	Cr £
Bank	....	....
Capital	....	....
Sales ledger control	....	....
Sales	....	....
Purchases ledger control	....	....
Purchases	....	....
Rent of premises	....	....
Payroll expenses	....	....
Travel expenses	....	....
General expenses	....	....
Equipment lease payments	....	....
Drawings	....	....
Vehicle	....	....
Vehicle – accumulated depreciation	....	....
Depreciation charge	....	....
Accrual	....	....
Prepayment	....	....
Bad debt written off	....	....
Total	....	....

Task 1.8

Before you prepare the final accounts for Jenny Shaw, you need to know more about the equipment lease payments paid from the bank account. You need to know whether she has taken out an operating lease or a finance lease.

Draft an e-mail to Jenny Shaw which:

*   **explains why it is important for you to know which type of lease it is.**

*   **explains the differences between an operating lease and a finance lease.**

*   **asks her to confirm which type of lease she has taken out.**

If you need more space, please use a separate piece of paper.

From:	A Student
To:	Jenny Shaw
Date:	 2007
Subject:	Equipment lease payments

Task 1.9

As Jenny Shaw's business grows, she will have to make decisions about accounting policies. FRS 18 names four objectives which should be considered when selecting accounting policies.

Name two of the objectives listed in FRS 18 which should be considered when selecting accounting policies.

_____

_____

SECTION 2

You should spend about 100 minutes on this section.

DATA

Henry and James are the owners of HJ Cleaning, a partnership business that sells industrial cleaning equipment.

You are an accounting technician at Harper and Co, the accounting firm that prepares the final accounts for HJ Cleaning.

*   The financial year end is 31 March.

*   The partners maintain an integrated accounting system consisting of a main ledger, a purchases ledger, a sales ledger and a stock ledger.

*   Stock records are maintained at cost in the stock ledger which is updated every time a sale or stock purchase is made.

*   HJ Cleaning is registered for VAT.

*   The proforma extended trial balance for the year ended 31 March 2007 is on pages 130 and 131.

At the end of the financial year on 31 March 2007, the following trial balance was taken from the main ledger:

	Dr £	Cr £
Administration expenses	88,014	
Bank	106,571	
Capital account – Henry		50,000
Capital account – James		50,000
Cash	165	
Closing stock	69,580	69,580
Current account – Henry		3,600
Current account – James		4,200
Depreciation charge for the year	8,750	
Opening stock	75,150	
Purchases	185,400	
Purchases ledger control account		16,200
Rent	14,000	
Sales		450,800
Sales ledger control account	53,000	
Selling expenses	43,970	
VAT		10,220
Vehicles at cost	35,000	
Vehicles accumulated depreciation		25,000
Total	679,600	679,600

ADDITIONAL DATA

Most of the year-end adjustments have been entered, but there are some adjustments you now need to make:

(a)   Accountancy fees of £1,900 need to be accrued. Ignore VAT.

(b)   A provision for doubtful debts of 1.5% of the value of the sales ledger control account needs to be introduced.

(c)   The total value of a purchase invoice for electricity for £329, including VAT of 17.5%, was debited to selling expenses. Electricity should be charged to administration expenses.

(d)   A credit note from a supplier for purchases was entered into the ledgers as a purchase invoice. The credit note was for £470 including VAT at 17.5%.

Task 2.1

Prepare journal entries to account for the above, using the blank journal below.   Dates and narratives are not required. There is space for workings on the next page.

JOURNAL

	Dr £	Cr £

Workings

Task 2.2

Enter your journal entries into the adjustment columns of the extended trial balance on page 131.

Task 2.3

Entend the profit and loss and balance sheet columns of the extended trial balance on page 131. Make entries to record the net profit or loss for the year ended 31 March 2007.

HJ Cleaning – Extended Trial Balance

	Ledger balances	
	Dr £	Cr £
Administration expenses	88,014	
Bank	106,571	
Capital account – Henry		50,000
Capital account – James		50,000
Cash	165	
Closing stock	69,580	69,580
Current account – Henry		3,600
Current account – James		4,200
Depreciation charge for the year	8,750	
Opening stock	75,150	
Purchases	185,400	
Purchases ledger control account		16,200
Rent	14,000	
Sales		450,800
Sales ledger control account	53,000	
Selling expenses	43,970	
VAT		10,220
Vehicles at cost	35,000	
Vehicles accumulated depreciation		25,000
TOTAL	679,600	679,600

as at 31 March 2007

Adjustments		Profit and Loss Account		Balance Sheet	
Dr £	Cr £	Dr £	Cr £	Dr £	Cr £

ADDITIONAL DATA

Henry and James share the profits of the partnership equally.

Task 2.4

Update the partners' current accounts to account for the profit or loss for the year ended 31 March 2007. Balance off the accounts and bring the balances down.

Current Accounts

2007		Henry £	James £	2007		Henry £	James £
				31 Mar	Balance b/d	3,600	4,200

Task 2.5

Prepare a balance sheet for HJ Cleaning as at 31 March 2007.

Workings	HJ Cleaning Balance Sheet as at 31 March 2007	£	£	£
	Fixed Assets			
	Vehicles			
	Current Assets			
	Stock			
	Debtors			
	Bank			
	Cash			
	Current Liabilities			
	Creditors			
	VAT			
	Accruals			
	Net current assets			
	Net assets			
	Capital Employed	Henry	James	Total
	Capital accounts			
	Current accounts			
	Total			

ADDITIONAL DATA

On 1 April 2007 Charles was admitted to the partnership.

- He introduced £100,000 to the bank account.

- Goodwill was valued at £220,000 on 31 March 2007.

- Goodwill is to be eliminated from the accounts.

- The new profit sharing percentages are:

    Henry   40%

    James   40%

    Charles   20%

Task 2.6

Update the capital accounts for the partnership, showing clearly the introduction and elimination of goodwill. Balance off the accounts.

Capital Accounts

		Henry	James	Charles			Henry	James	Charles
2007		£	£	£	2007		£	£	£
					1 Apr	Balance b/d	50,000	50,000	

Task 2.7

Your uncle is a good friend of Charles, the new partner at HJ Cleaning. He knows you are involved in preparing the accounts for the partnership. He asks you how much money Charles has invested in HJ Cleaning.

How should you respond to your uncle's question?

_____

_____

_____

_____

_____

Practice Examination 5
Fixit; Dawson Partnerhip

Element coverage

5.1 maintaining records relating to capital acquisition and disposal

5.2 collecting and collating information for the preparation of final accounts

5.3 preparing the final accounts of sole traders and partnerships

Suggested time allocation

Three hours plus 15 minutes' reading time.

PRACTICE EXAMINATION 5
FIXIT; DAWSON PARTNERSHIP

This Examination is in two sections.

You have to show competence in both sections.

You should therefore attempt and aim to complete every task in both sections.

You should spend about 80 minutes on section 1, and 100 minutes on section 2.

SECTION 1

You should spend about 80 minutes on this section.

DATA

Frank Khan owns Fixit, a business that repairs and maintains properties. There are no credit sales. The business operates from small rented premises where the plant and equipment are stored.

Frank Khan does not keep a double entry bookkeeping system.

You are an accounting technician at Harper and Co, the accounting firm that prepares the final accounts for Fixit. You are working on the accounts for Fixit for the year ending 31 October 2007. Your colleague has already summarised the cash and bank accounts, which are shown on the next page.

Fixit

Cash and Bank summary for the year ended 31 October 2007

	Cash	Bank		Cash	Bank
	£	£		£	£
Balances b/d	560	2,310	Rent		2,600
Sales	17,400	32,000	Wages	20,500	
Bank	10,000		Materials	2,600	
			Creditors for materials		11,005
			Travel expenses	2,470	
			Administration expenses	1,990	
			Cash		10,000
			Balances c/d	400	10,705
	27,960	34,310		27,960	34,310

The following balances are also available:

Assets and liabilities as at:	31 October 2006	31 October 2007
	£	£
Plant and equipment at cost	19,000	19,000
Plant and equipment accumulated depreciation	5,600	Not yet available
Stocks of materials at cost	2,890	1,940
Prepayment for rent	550	Not yet available
Creditors for materials	1,720	1,835
Accrual for travel expenses	380	425

Task 1.1

Calculate the figure for capital as at 31 October 2006.

_____

_____

_____

_____

_____

_____

_____

_____

_____

_____

_____

_____

Task 1.2

Calculate the total sales for the year ended 31 October 2007.

_____

_____

_____

_____

Task 1.3

Prepare the purchases ledger control account for the year ended 31 October 2007, showing clearly the credit purchases of materials.

Purchases ledger control account

	£		£

Task 1.4

Calculate the total purchases of materials for the year ended 31 October 2007.

_____

_____

_____

Task 1.5

Depreciation is provided at 25% per annum on a reducing balance basis.

(a)   Calculate the depreciation charge for the year ended 31 October 2007.

_____

_____

_____

_____

_____

(b) Calculate the revised accumulated depreciation as at 31 October 2007.

_____

_____

_____

_____

_____

Task 1.6

Calculate the travel expenses for the year ended 31 October 2007.

_____

_____

_____

_____

_____

Task 1.7

The figure for rent in the cash and bank summary on page 137 includes £650 for the quarter starting 1 November 2007.

Prepare the rent account for the year ended 31 October 2007, showing clearly the rent for the year.

Rent

	£		£

Task 1.8

Frank Khan has given you a closing stock figure of £1,940 at cost. He has also told you that he has a supply of bricks which he acquired free of charge. He is confident that he will be able to sell these bricks for at least £500. These are not included in the stock valuation of £1,940.

What figure for closing stock should be included in the accounts of Fixit?

(Circle only one answer)

£1,440   /   £1,940   /   £2,440   /   **None of these**

Task 1.9

Complete the trial balance below as at 31 October 2007, taking into account your answers to the above tasks, and all the other information you have been given.

Fixit
Trial balance as at 31 October 2007

	Dr £	Cr £
Plant and equipment		
Plant and equipment accumulated depreciation		
Opening stock		
Prepayment		
Creditors for materials		
Accrual		
Bank		
Cash		
Capital		
Sales		
Purchases		
Wages		
Depreciation charge for the year		
Travel expenses		
Rent		
Administration expenses		
Closing stock – profit and loss account		
Closing stock – balance sheet		
Total		

Task 1.10

Frank Khan has told you he is concerned about the figure in the trial balance for fixed assets. He knows that it includes all the plant and equipment that he has bought over a number of years but he does not have a list of the items. It is possible that some are broken or missing. He needs your advice.

Write a memo to Frank Khan:

- **List SIX items of information that a fixed assets register should contain.**

- **Give THREE reasons why he should keep a fixed assets register.**

MEMO
To: **Frank Khan**
From: **A Student**
Subject: **Fixed Assets Register**
Date: 2007

SECTION 2

You should spend about 100 minutes on this section.

DATA

Dan, Kim and Ted are the owners of Dawson, a partnership business that sells building supplies to the building trade.

You are an accounting technician at Harper and Co, the accounting firm that prepares the final accounts for Dawson.

- The financial year end is 31 October.

- The partners maintain a double entry accounting system consisting of a main ledger, a purchases ledger, and a sales ledger.

- Dawson is registered for VAT.

- The trial balance for the year ended 31 October 2007 is shown on the next page.

Dawson – Trial balance as at 31 October 2007

	Ledger balances	
	Dr £	Cr £
Administration expenses	18,712	
Bank	35,459	
Capital account: as at 1 November 2006 – Dan		25,000
Capital account: as at 1 November 2006 – Kim		25,000
Capital account: as at 1 November 2006 – Ted		25,000
Cash	2,500	
Closing stock – balance sheet	68,950	
Closing stock – profit and loss account		68,950
Current account – Dan	20,000	
Current account – Kim	30,000	
Current account – Ted	30,000	
Equipment at cost	35,000	
Equipment accumulated depreciation		12,576
Opening stock	70,200	
Purchases	432,500	
Purchases ledger control account		70,350
Rent	15,000	
Sales		585,700
Sales ledger control account	41,071	
Suspense	9,200	
VAT		7,350
Wages	11,334	
TOTAL	**819,926**	**819,926**

DATA

You have investigated the balance on the suspense account. You have discovered some errors that now need to be corrected. There are also some year-end adjustments to be made:

(a)   Some equipment was scrapped during the year:

Original cost	£2,000
Net book value at the time of disposal	£1,024
Proceeds	Nil

(b)   Depreciation needs to be provided for the equipment at 20% using the reducing balance method. No depreciation is provided in the year of disposal.

(c)   A vehicle costing £8,500 was purchased on 31 October 2007. The correct entry was made to the bank, but no other entries were made. No depreciation needs to be provided for the year ended 31 October 2007.

(d)   The figures from the columns of the sales day book for 15 October have been totalled correctly as follows:

Sales column	£2,000
VAT column	£350
Total column	£2,350

The amounts have been posted as follows:

Dr Sales ledger control account	£2,000	
Cr VAT		£350
Cr Sales		£2,350

(e)   An amount for the purchase of goods of £756 net of VAT has been debited to the opening stock account.

Task 2.1

Prepare journal entries to account for items (a) to (e). Use the blank journal on the next page. Dates and narratives are not required.

JOURNAL

	Dr £	Cr £

Workings

Task 2.2

Prepare a profit and loss account for the partnership for the year ended 31 October 2007, showing clearly the gross profit and the net profit. Use the trial balance from page 144 and your journal adjustments from page 146.

Workings			

ADDITIONAL DATA

On 30 June 2007, Dan retired from the partnership. You have the following information about the partnership agreement:

- Partners' annual salaries

Dan	£30,000	(£20,000 for the period to 30 June 2007)
Kim	£30,000	
Ted	£30,000	

- Interest on capital accounts

  3% per annum on the balances at the beginning of the year

- Profit share, effective until 30 June 2007

Dan	40%
Kim	30%
Ted	30%

- Profit share, effective from 1 July 2007

Kim	50%
Ted	50%

You can assume that profits accrued evenly during the year.

Workings

Task 2.3

Prepare the appropriation account for the partnership for the year ended 31 October 2007.

ADDITIONAL DATA

*   Goodwill was valued at £100,000 on 30 June 2007.

*   Goodwill is to be eliminated from the accounts.

Task 2.4

Prepare the goodwill account for the partnership for the year ended 31 October 2007. Show clearly the individual transfers to each of the partners' capital accounts.

Goodwill Account

Date		£	Date		£

Task 2.5

There is not enough cash available to settle Dan's interest in the partnership immediately. The partners have agreed to settle Dan's interest by the introduction of a loan.

(a) **Which one of the following would be the correct journal entry to clear Dan's capital account to the loan account? Tick the correct box. (✓).**

☐ Dr Capital – Dan   Cr Loan – Dan

☐ Dr Loan – Dan   Cr Capital – Dan

☐ Dr Capital – Dan   Cr Bank

☐ Dr Bank   Cr Capital – Dan

(b) **When the balance sheet of Dawson is drawn up, in which section will the balance on Dan's loan account be shown? Tick the correct box. (✓).**

☐ Assets

☐ Liabilities

☐ Capital

Task 2.6

The closing stock figure included in the trial balance on page 144 was taken from the stock ledger cards which are updated when stock is received or issued. The partners of Dawson inform you that there are often differences between the quantity written on the stock cards and the physical stock actually counted.

Draft a note to the partners of Dawson. In your note:

• **List THREE reasons why the stock cards and the physical stock might not agree.**

• **Explain why it is important to regularly reconcile the stock records with the physical stock.**

Appendix:
photocopiable resources

These pages may be photocopied for student use, but remain the copyright of the author. It is recommended that they are enlarged to A4 size.

These pages are also available for download from the Resources Section of www.osbornebooks.co.uk

The forms and formats include:

Dr   Cr

Date	Details	Amount	Date	Details	Amount
		£			£

Dr   Cr

Date	Details	Amount	Date	Details	Amount
		£			£

Dr   Cr

Date	Details	Amount	Date	Details	Amount
		£			£

JOURNAL

Details	Dr £	Cr £

EXTENDED TRIAL BALANCE

name.......... date..........

EXTENDED TRIAL BALANCE	Ledger balances		Adjustments		Profit and loss		Balance sheet	
Account name	Dr £	Cr £	Dr £	Cr £	Dr £	Cr £	Dr £	Cr £
Closing stock: Profit and loss								
Closing stock: Balance sheet								
Accruals								
Prepayments								
Depreciation								
Bad debts								
Provision for doubtful debts:adjustment								
Net profit/loss								

FIXED ASSET REGISTER PAGE

EXTRACT FROM FIXED ASSET REGISTER

Description/serial no	Date acquired	Original cost £	Depreciation £	NBV £	Funding method	Disposal proceeds £	Disposal date

SOLE TRADER: TRADING AND PROFIT AND LOSS ACCOUNT

This example layout for final accounts is for sole trader businesses; for partnerships, the layout will need to be adjusted to take note of the partners' capital and current accounts).

TRADING AND PROFIT AND LOSS ACCOUNT OF .... **(name)**
FOR THE YEAR/PERIOD ENDED ....**(date)**

	£	£	£
Sales			......
Less Sales returns			......
Net sales			...... (a)
Opening stock		......	
Purchases	......		
Carriage in	......		
Less Purchases returns	......		
Net purchases		......	
		......	
Less Closing stock		......	
Cost of sales			...... (b)
Gross profit (a) – (b)			...... (c)
Add other income, eg			
Discount received			......
Provision for doubtful debts (reduction)			...... ⎤ (d)
Profit on sale of fixed assets			......
Other income			...... ⎦
(c) + (d)			...... (e)
Less overheads, eg			
Vehicle running expenses		......	
Rent		......	
Rates		......	
Heating and lighting		......	
Telephone		......	
Salaries and wages		......	
Discount allowed		......	
Carriage out		......	
Depreciation		......	
Loss on sale of fixed assets		......	
Bad debts written off		......	
Provision for doubtful debts (increase)		......	
			...... (f)
Net profit (e) – (f)			...... (g)

SOLE TRADER: BALANCE SHEET

BALANCE SHEET OF .... **(name) AS AT** .... **(date)**

	£	£	£	
Fixed assets	Cost (a)	Prov for dep'n (b)	Net	(a) – (b)
Intangible: Goodwill	......	......	......	
Tangible: Premises	......	......	......	
Equipment	......	......	......	
Vehicles	......	......	......	
etc	......	......	......	
	......	......	......	(c)
Current assets				
Stock (closing)		......		
Debtors	......			
Less provision for doubtful debts	......			
		......		
Prepayments		......		
Bank		......		
Cash		......		
		......		(d)
Less Current liabilities				
Creditors	......			
Accruals	......			
Bank overdraft	......			
		......		(e)
Working capital (or **Net current assets**) (d) – (e)			......	(f)
(c) + (f)			......	(g)
Less Long-term liabilities				
Loans			......	(h)
NET ASSETS (g) – (h)			......	(i)
FINANCED BY				
Capital				
Opening capital			......	
Add net profit (from profit and loss account)			......	
			......	
Less drawings			......	
			......	(i)

Note: balance sheet balances at points (i)

Practical point: When preparing handwritten final accounts it is usual practice to underline all the headings and sub-headings shown in bold print in the example layout.

MEMORANDUM

To:

From:

Subject:

Date: